D0807859

Can Laughter Make the World a Better Place?

Can Laughter Make the World a Better Place?

Shawn R. Tucker

WIPF & STOCK · Eugene, Oregon

CAN LAUGHTER MAKE THE WORLD A BETTER PLACE?

Wipf & Stock
An Imprint of Wipf and Stock Publishers
199 W. 8th Ave., Suite 3
Eugene, OR 97401

www.wipfandstock.com

PAPERBACK ISBN: 978-1-6667-3299-3
HARDCOVER ISBN: 978-1-6667-2720-3
EBOOK ISBN: 978-1-6667-2721-0

03/09/22

To Tina Marie, Sprite, Brycie Brycie Bear, My G, and Nicole

Contents

Figures

Acknowledgments

THANK YOU TO THOSE at Wipf and Stock who helped bring this project to fruition. Your professionalism and generosity were invaluable in the process. I'm also grateful for the many Elon University students who have taken my Aspects of Laughter and Laughter and the Humanities courses over the years. Your feedback on the chapters and your enthusiasm and insight into the material helped make this possible.

I also extend my deep gratitude to Elon University. This wonderful institution, where I'm proud to be able to teach and work, offered tremendous support for this project. That support included assistance to fund various parts of the research and publication process. Elon University provided me with the sabbatical during which much of this material was finally drafted.

Introduction

Warning: Chainsaw-Wielding Laser Sharks

THE OBSTACLE COURSE HAS a 13-foot climbing wall. And barbed wire. It also has quicksand and landmines. There is a greasy tightrope over a pool of shark-infested waters. And the sharks have chainsaws and lasers. What is this obstacle course? It is meeting your significant other's family for the first time, and there are so many ways it can go wrong.

I cannot tell you where all of the landmines or obstacles are, but I can warn you about one chainsaw-wielding laser shark: laughing at the family jokes. You are going to get with these people, and they all know each other. They will notice you, the new person, but after they get over you being there, they will resume being how they always are with each other. They might start to tease one another. They may say something odd like, "Oh, I have room for something cold." They will look at each other and laugh. You will not understand. They will tell you the story of the dinner where they went to someone's house and the little sister wanted some of the ice cream she noticed that the hosts had in their freezer. She was young at the time, and she thought she was being subtle when she said, "Ummm, I have a space for something cold." They will still think it is funny. It won't be funny to you—you were not there.

They are laughing and at ease with one another. This may trick you into getting comfortable. Don't get comfortable. As they chat and quip and tease, they might mention some funny and awkward or embarrassing story about the matriarch or patriarch or other senior and otherwise respected member of the family. The faint noise you should hear is the rattle of chainsaws firing up. They will tell this story with lots and lots of laughter, and you might find the story amusing. It might be very funny. You might want to laugh. Do not laugh. Do not even smile. The correct response to this situation is the following: shake your head slightly, darken your eyes, and reply thusly: "You should not say things like that about such a lovely person." Make a straight line of your mouth after you say this, and don't worry if they look at you like you are a stick in the mud. You might not realize it, but here you are given the choice between being a stick in the mud or being shark chum. Pick the stick.

The issue is this—when you are auditioning for the role of new member of the family, when do you get to laugh at the family jokes? Perhaps you have joined a family through marriage or otherwise, and you have dealt with this issue. It is difficult. What is fun is when someone new joins your family. You get to see them squirm as they try to figure out if they can smile about your mom's failed attempts at cooking or your dad's home improvement efforts that led to him being electrocuted three hilarious times. When is someone an outsider who should at least seem surprised that these people say such things about family members? When are you in? If you are part of the family, then of course you can participate in the joking and teasing, but as an outsider there is rarely a clear line telling you when you are in and when you are not yet in. Well, that is until you laugh at a joke, or worse, make a joke, only to realize that they still don't see you as in. You will know you are out because they will not laugh. The air will turn to lead or feel sucked out of the room. They will be hurt and uncomfortable. You will realize that the noise of splashing and chomping as well as the lasers and chainsaws are the sharks attacking you.

Family members make jokes that people outside of the family cannot make. Joking and teasing can strengthen bonds of affection and love. Those same jokes can feel demeaning when there is distance or hostility instead of affection. Laughing *with* loved ones adds to life's joy and richness. Laughing *at* enemies is a cutting, destructive weapon.

Laughter is contradictory, and the following chapters examine many of those contradictions. We'll examine laughter in movies like *Zombieland* and *Dr. Strangelove*, and in television shows like *Malcolm in the Middle*. We'll look at laughter in novels like *A Confederacy of Dunces* and *The Sellout*, as well as in art by Picasso and the Guerrilla Girls. We'll blend in remarkable insights about laughter from psychologists, social scientists, neuroscientists, philosophers, and political activists. We'll spend time with the works of a contemporary Moroccan photographer, with an undocumented immigrant and his daughter, and with a branch manager who believes he is the world's best boss. We'll see people use laughter as they respond to the police, as they contend with political opponents, and as they deal with trauma—their own trauma or the trauma of loved ones.

All of this will show how laughter does not make the world a better place. It will show how laughter demeans and divides. It will explore how laughter occasionally raises useful questions. Sometimes laughter helps us be more self-aware and more self-critical. Sometimes it creates a unique space to learn and question, and sometimes it connects us with others. But not always. It could be that sometimes laughter makes the world a better place. Maybe. And some laughter invites you to be your best self. It draws out the best in others, it uses delight to lead you out of ugly attitudes and prejudices, and it strengthens family and friendship bonds. In these ways, laughter makes the world a better place.

If nothing else, this book will help you avoid at least one chainsaw-wielding laser shark if you simply remember this phrase—"You should not say things like that about such a lovely person."

No

CHAPTER 1

Popular 1970s Television Show or
Human Resources Training Video?

Ben and Franklin

HOURS OF WORKING TO keep critically wounded soldiers alive have left Ben glassy-eyed and spent. He collapses on his army-issue cot. He has just enough energy to open a letter from the college where he graduated many years ago. Ben's exhausted face lights up as he looks the letter over. His eyes twinkle as he reads it to the other doctor who shares a tent with him. The letter explains that the college likes his idea and kind gesture, and they will support him. Ben had previously written to the dean of his alma mater to see if they would admit a domestic worker who had been assisting Ben and his colleagues. Ben's boyish grin begins to fade as he tries to figure out the logistics of getting a Korean man to the United States and paying for his tuition. His parents will be willing to provide housing. Faced with the dilemma of raising around $2,000, a sly smile moves across his face. He asks his friend what the people in his mobile army surgical hospital want. They agree that everyone wants booze and sex. The doctors plan a party with a raffle to raise the money that they need to send Ho-Jon to the United States.

Another surgeon at the same unit snaps at an attending nurse for giving him the wrong item. She responds that she gave him what he asked for, only for him to reply that she should have given him what he needed,

3

not what he requested. This surgeon, Franklin, shares a tent with Ben, but the two doctors are very different. Franklin is shorter, not nearly as witty, and has unattractive, sharp, foxlike facial features. Franklin's disapproving face sometimes erupts in short fits of high-pitched, clawing laughter. Franklin, besides blaming others for his mistakes, especially underlings, lacks Ben's surgical skills. Franklin has a cherished Bible, but his Bible study is self-righteous and hypocritical. The married Franklin has an ongoing relationship with another woman, someone who is also bitter, demanding, and generally disliked. Franklin will inevitably oppose Ben's kind-hearted efforts to help Ho-Jon.

Though Ben and Franklin work in the same Korean mobile army surgical hospital, they do not get along. At all. Ben is willing to go around or even ignore rules if doing so allows him to help others, but the sanctimonious and rule-oriented Franklin is the kind of killjoy who seems determined to get in his way and, in the process, make everyone miserable. Oh, and two more things—Ben and Franklin happened to be two of the most important masculine role models in my life, and neither one is a real person.

I was born in the United States in the late sixties. On September 17, 1972, I was almost four years old. That was the day television was introduced to Capt. Benjamin Franklin "Hawkeye" Pierce and Major Franklin Delano Marian Burns, two central characters in the show *M*A*S*H*.[1] This show would air in prime time until February 28, 1983. I don't think I saw much of the show in prime time, since it tended to come on after my bedtime. Still, during my formative years in the 70s and 80s, *M*A*S*H* was on in syndication. I recall the show being on after school, and during the summer it was on more than once a day. It seems to me that I must have watched every episode at least once.

In every episode, I was rooting for Hawkeye. He was the skillful, clever, and good-natured one who wanted to do something good, or at least relax after doing his demanding job. And of course I rooted against Frank. The man with the nickname "Ferret Face" was everything I wanted to avoid. All of this is evident in the show's very first, or "Pilot," episode. The episode begins with a voiceover of Hawkeye talking to his father about the demands of working in an army field hospital. He speaks in a somber, serious manner about how field surgeons do all that they can to keep the young soldiers alive. During the voiceover we see Hawkeye and Frank performing surgery on those soldiers. Hawkeye is serious and skillful, while Frank blames a

1. See Reynolds, *M*A*S*H*.

nurse for his own mistake. Hawkeye rebukes Frank for his outburst. Soon after, Frank confronts him outside the surgical tent. Right from the start of the very first episode, Frank comes off as the domineering and petty contrast to the charming and above-it-all Hawkeye.

The episode's central conflict is Hawkeye's efforts to raise the money for Ho-Jon. Hawkeye and Trapper plan a party that will raise that money, as well as give everyone in the camp a chance to relax and unwind. They arrange a raffle for a weekend pass to Tokyo that will include the company of an attractive nurse, but Hawkeye will work it out so that the priest, Father Mulcahy, will win.

A scuffle between Hawkeye and Frank in the tent they share is the first obstacle in Hawkeye's plan. The camp's commanding officer, Lt. Col. Henry Blake, is forced to cancel the fundraising party as a response to Frank's complaints. When Hawkeye and Trapper find out that Blake will be away, they plan on ignoring Blake's orders and having the party in his absence. Here again Frank blocks their efforts to help Ho-Jon. As Frank is left in charge during Henry's absence, he cancels all camp activities. Hawkeye manages to get some of the other hospital personnel to help him sedate Frank so that they can hold the party. The party is very successful, until Gen. Hammond arrives. The head nurse and Frank's love interest, Margaret Houlihan, notified Gen. Hammond about what was going on. But at the very moment that Gen. Hammond is going to arrest Hawkeye and Trapper, helicopters arrive with injured Canadian soldiers. Hawkeye and Trapper invite Gen. Hammond, a doctor himself, to help attend to those soldiers. After hours of intense surgery, Gen. Hammond is so impressed with Hawkeye's ability that he decides not to arrest or charge him for the fundraising party. In the general's view, Hawkeye is just too valuable to the hospital to let such a petty infraction take him from the facility's essential work.

Persuasive Laughter

Hawkeye's surgical skills get him off the hook with Gen. Hammond, but it isn't just Hawkeye's gifts as a surgeon that make him so influential. In fact, to talk about Hawkeye's power, we can look at something that happened in October of 1984—the presidential debate between former Vice President Walter Mondale and former California Governor Ronald Reagan. Before the debate, there were questions about Reagan's mental fitness for the job. Reagan did something unexpected to counter those fears. The former governor delivered a series of preplanned and brilliant one-liners. An example is something Reagan said about his age: "I will not make age an issue of this campaign. I am not going to exploit, for political purposes, my opponent's youth and inexperience."[2]

This story and example are funny, but they might be difficult to connect with Hawkeye. In Matthew Lieberman's book *Social: Why Our Brains Are Wired to Connect*, Lieberman uses Reagan's jokes as an example to show how socially connected we are. Reagan won the debate, but for Lieberman the reason is unexpected. Lieberman puts it this way: "Reagan himself didn't change our minds about him. It took a few hundred people in the audience to change our minds. It was their laughter coming over the airwaves that moved the needle on how we viewed Reagan."[3]

To develop this idea that it was the laughter of a few hundred people that made the difference, Lieberman notes the work of social psychologist Steve Fein. Fein compared the responses of people who heard Reagan's lines with the audience's laughter against those who heard the lines without the laughter. Those who heard the laughter concluded that Reagan outperformed Mondale. Those who heard Reagan without the laughter reached the opposite conclusion—that Mondale outperformed Reagan. Lieberman draws this conclusion: "We didn't think Reagan was funny because Reagan was funny. We thought Reagan was funny because a small group of strangers in the audience thought Reagan was funny. We were influenced by innocuous social cues."[4]

Lieberman says that most of us believe that we would not be influenced so easily. As Lieberman puts it, "We like to think of ourselves as independent-minded and immune to this sort of influence. Yet we would be wrong. Every day others influence us in countless ways that we do not recognize or appreciate."[5] Lieberman's entire book is about how we are social beings with brains wired to connect with those around us.

Part of Hawkeye's strong influence over the people in the camp is his humor. When Frank confronts Hawkeye after surgery within the first five minutes of the show's first episode, Hawkeye makes a joke. Frank accuses Hawkeye of a lack of professionalism as an officer and a doctor. Hawkeye replies, "Frank, I happen to be an officer only because I foolishly

2. Lieberman, *Social*, 6.

3. Lieberman, *Social*, 6.

4. Lieberman, *Social*, 6–7.

5. Lieberman, *Social*, 7.

opened an invitation from President Truman to come to this costume party."[6] Hawkeye then challenges Frank to a duel, but instead of swords or pistols, they will fight with specimen bottles. Hawkeye defuses Frank's attacks while making Frank look foolish and humorless. Hawkeye's jokes, like Reagan's, reveal his quick mind and mental fitness, while also beating out a less witty opponent. Laughter is key to why we are influenced and persuaded by Hawkeye and Reagan.

Sticks and Stones

Lieberman talks about laughter because it can be such a powerful social cue. He notes that current neuroscience research indicates that physical pain and social rejection register in similar ways in the same part of the brain. Lieberman poses this question: "Ask yourself what have been one or two of the most painful experiences of your life. Did you think of the physical pain of a broken leg or really bad fall?"[7] Lieberman then guesses that at least one of those very painful experiences will be social pain, such as the loss of a loved one, being rejected by a romantic partner, or experiencing public humiliation. The neuroscientist asks and then answers, "Why do we associate such events with the word pain? When human beings experience threats or damages to their social bonds, the brain responds in much the same way it responds to physical pain."[8]

One interesting note about physical pain and social pain is what Lieberman says about bullying. He notes that, "From a young age, we teach children to say, 'Sticks and stones will break my bones, but names will never hurt me.'"[9] Lieberman's research shows that that is not true. Bullying is so damaging, "not because one individual is rejecting us but because we tend to believe that the bully speaks for others."[10] When no one steps in to help the victim, then that "absence of support is taken as a sign of mass rejection."[11] Brains that are built to connect with others experience bullying as painful, large-scale rejection.

---

6. Reynolds, *M*A*S*H*, 4:19–4:26.
7. Lieberman, *Social*, 40.
8. Lieberman, *Social*, 40.
9. Lieberman, *Social*, 69.
10. Lieberman, *Social*, 69.
11. Lieberman, *Social*, 69.

Oh, and By the Way, Hawkeye is a . . .

For all of his good looks, charm, and wit, when we look back at *M*A*S*H*'s pilot episode, we see that Hawkeye bullies Frank. Toward the middle of the episode, when Hawkeye and Trapper see that their fundraising is coming up short, Hawkeye notes that Frank has not contributed. Frank is not in the tent that the surgeons share, so Hawkeye goes through Frank's belongings, including his Bible, to steal from him. I don't know how it feels for you to have a roommate or someone else, especially someone who actively dislikes and disrespects you, go through your stuff, but when Frank arrives and sees what's going on, he is very upset. In his rage, Frank screams about Hawkeye and Trapper's snide remarks before tearing down pictures in the tent and grabbing their prized distillery. Cornered by Hawkeye and Trapper, Frank ends up throwing the distillery to the ground. Hawkeye and Trapper then team up to put a sack over Frank and kick him out of the tent. Throughout the exchange, Frank's rage is met with Hawkeye's condescending, snide laughter.

The episode's most humorous and compelling example of how Hawkeye bullies Frank comes after Col. Blake leaves. Blake canceled the fundraising party before he left. Frank, who is the next senior officer and in charge while Blake is gone, tries to carry out Blake's order. But Hawkeye manages to get Frank sedated so that he can hold the party. He does this by first tricking Frank into leaning over to listen to a patient. The physically vulnerable Frank is then injected in the butt with a powerful, fast-acting sedative. Woozy, jazzlike music accompanies the scene of the now-woozy Frank. Hawkeye and several other people make jokes at Frank's expense as they bandage him up and hide him away in a bed. Hawkeye jokingly tells all in attendance that the "patient" is to be sedated every hour on the hour.

Hawkeye does not sedate Frank alone. Instead, a dozen or so camp personnel actively conspire to incapacitate the camp's acting commanding officer. Hawkeye has enough power at the facility to take it over. The scene itself, the music, Frank's response, and Hawkeye's jokes create a powerful appeal to the show's audience. The people in the camp and the people watching the show are charmed by the bully's power, his boyish smile, and his quick wit.

We see Hawkeye's power and laughter again when the concerned head nurse, Margaret Houlihan, frantically searches for the missing Frank. She is visibly anxious as she asks Hawkeye about Frank's whereabouts. Hawkeye responds to her anxiety with dismissive, snide jokes. Hawkeye maneuvers Margaret with the same wit, charm, and power he used against Frank.

Even when Margaret finds Frank, Hawkeye makes Margaret's distress seem comical. When Frank staggers back with Margaret to what remains of the party, Hawkeye mockingly calls Frank "The Mummy."[12]

Hawkeye's power, a power that comes in part because of his quick wit, seems innocent and good natured. No one wants to be Frank or Margaret, and everybody in the camp, as well as the television viewers, wants to be on Hawkeye's side. But Hawkeye doesn't use his powers for good. Hawkeye creates a hostile work environment for two of the most important people in this army field hospital. His power forces everyone to line up on his side or face the possibility that he will also bully them.

Hawkeye's dismissive and condescending attitude toward Margaret matches his abusive treatment of other women at the camp.[13] This is evident in how he treats Lt. Dish. When Hawkeye and Trapper pitch their fundraising idea to Col. Blake, Blake asks them which nurse they have conned into going to Tokyo for two days with the raffle winner. The assumption is that a male winner will get two days of sexual access to the nurse. The generic term for an arrangement like this is prostitution, but Hawkeye is so charming that one could be lulled into rejecting the frank and accurate label.

When Hawkeye answers Blake's question about who will be the prostituted medical and military professional, we see a montage of scenes with Hawkeye's voiceover and a musical accompaniment. This montage features scene-after-scene of Hawkeye attempting to . . . okay, I don't know how people in the seventies would have described what he's attempting to do. Is he trying to charm her? Is he trying to seduce her? Let's see.

The montage's pattern is to first show Lt. Dish alone, engaged in private activities like painting her toenails, looking for a book in a camp library, flipping through a magazine, reading, and, last, but certainly not least, showering. In each instance, after she is first shown alone, a smiling and frisky Hawkeye suddenly appears. A smooth jazzlike variation on the show's theme plays quietly over the scenes. In Hawkeye's voiceover, he claims his lips were made by Stradivarius. Kissing her, he puns on her last name when he tells her he will answer her questions after he finishes his lunch. To rebuff Hawkeye's advances, Lt. Dish reminds him that she's engaged. He uses a joke to dismiss this. She complains that he invades her privacy and sneaks up on her. Another joke dismisses these allegations. She tells him that she is trying to be faithful but that "a girl can only take

---

12. Reynolds, *M*A*S*H*, 20:35.

13. See Wittebols, *Watching M*A*S*H, Watching America*.

so much."[14] More jokes and dismissals. Hawkeye's wit and charm show how humor, pestering, and an unwillingness to listen to a woman transform rejection into consent. "No" does not mean no—it means "use humor and charm to keep trying to get what I'm telling you I don't want to give." Of course that is not what the montage actually shows. The montage shows this: Hawkeye, the powerful doctor, is a sexual predator who refuses to hear a woman, his subordinate, when she says no. Hawkeye uses his power and laughter to rape her.

When I rewatched *M*A*S*H* for this chapter, I thought about my son-in-law. Okay, that might have sounded wrong. My son-in-law is currently getting a Master's degree in human resources. I thought of him because the "Pilot" episode seems like a human resources training video. I can imagine the questionnaire that human resources officers would use after showing this episode—"After watching the video, discuss workplace bullying. List at least three ways that this doctor creates a toxic work environment. Describe as many elements as you can of sexual harassment in this show, including the power dynamics." Somewhere on the questionnaire or training session or at least in the company handbook it should say, "Company Policy Strictly Prohibits Prostituting Coworkers."

One final note: Hawkeye's bullying, abusive laughter jeopardizes the lives of injured soldiers. The hostile work environment that Hawkeye creates for Frank and Margaret will not make them better medical professionals. This environment will make them anxious. It will rob them of confidence they will need to be quick and decisive. It will do the same for other medical professionals at the camp, especially if they don't fall in line with such a powerful bully. Raped and traumatized nurses will be less effective. And Hawkeye, for all of his seeming altruism in helping Ho-Jon, is not a good leader. The money for Ho-Jon's US college education is paid for with alcohol and prostitution. On the evening when Blake is gone, Hawkeye still holds the booze-soaked fundraising party even though he knows that the hospital will very soon be flooded with injured Canadian soldiers. Hawkeye wants his party, his fun, and his chance to show off his power even if it makes the medical staff less alert and less capable. Hawkeye's laughter is bullying, toxic, sexually harassing, predatory, selfish, and life-threatening. That laughter does not make the world a better place.

A personal reason why this is a big deal is because, growing up, Hawkeye was such a hero for me. Hawkeye was exactly what I wanted to be. I

14. Reynolds, *M*A*S*H*, 10:35.

remember having a conversation with my wife many years later. We were talking about what makes somebody cool or charming. I said that cool or charming people are often quick-witted. I told her that in my mind they were tremendously skillful at something important. Cool people were so skillful that they made it seem like they didn't care that they were brilliant. And Hawkeye is a brilliant surgeon. The "Pilot" episode is not the only episode where Hawkeye's surgical skills become a "Get-out-of-Consequences-Free Card." Hawkeye's skills are like a magic wand that he can wave and make disappear anything that threatens his power and charm. This power—Hawkeye's quick wit, tremendous social influence, and brilliant medical skills—became, in my mind, the ideal of masculinity. Hawkeye was the sort of man I pictured when I thought of someone cool and charming.

Luckily, life, experience, and the example of great men like my dad have let me see Hawkeye's version of masculinity for what it is—a toxic fraud.

CHAPTER 2

The Joke that Led to a 10 Percent Merit Pay Cut

RYAN IS STILL CHUCKLING to himself as he sits down at his desk. While he likes his job, Ryan is not looking forward to spending his afternoon deciding what employees will get merit pay raises. A small bright spot for him, as he plops down in his chair, comes from thinking about the punchline to the joke that Dan told him in the elevator on the way back from lunch. Ryan and Dan did not have lunch together, but they got into the same crowded after-lunch elevator. More and more people got off the elevator on the lower floors until it was just Ryan and Dan. Once the last person got off and the doors closed, Dan asked Ryan if he'd heard the joke about the guy and the girl stuck in the elevator. Ryan smiled back and said that he had not. Dan said, "a man and a woman were stranded in an elevator and they knew they were not going to get out alive. The woman turned to the man and said, 'make me feel like a woman before I die.' So the guy took off his clothes and said, 'Fold them!'" Ryan laughed at the joke's unexpected conclusion and continued to laugh periodically that afternoon.

If Ryan, in our hypothetical story, is making merit pay decisions for the company's male and female employees, do you think that the joke Ryan heard in the elevator could impact his decisions? One would obviously hope not. But, if Ryan already had some sexist views, is it possible that the joke could activate or release Ryan's views? And is it possible to scientifically measure if the joke and his sexist views could impact his decisions?

How Much Would You Donate?

This question of whether sexist jokes might impact behavior is the core of some ingenious laughter research. Thomas Ford, Christie Boxer, Jacob Armstrong, and Jessica Edel set out to test just that: Could sexist jokes prompt sexist behavior?[1] The researchers ended up creating two complementary experiments to see if sexist jokes might have real-world consequences.

For the first experiment, researchers began by giving a group of students something they called a "Social Attitudes Survey." What they really gave them was the "Ambivalent Sexism Inventory," a survey that researchers use to measure peoples' sexist attitudes. When participants complete the survey, they can mark a range of responses from "strongly disagree" to "strongly agree." They mark how much they agree or disagree with statements like this: "women seek to gain power by getting control over men" and "many women are actually seeking special favors, such as hiring policies that favor them over men, under the guise of asking for equality." This survey gives researchers a sense of where each participant lands between being high to low in hostile sexist attitudes.

The next step was to see if laughter might activate sexist attitudes. To measure laughter's impact, the first thing researchers did was give students time so that they would not see any connection between the Social Attitudes Survey and the second part of the experiment. After giving students a two-to-four-week buffer, researchers told students that they would participate in something vague and bland—a study of perceptions of social interactions and communication behavior. They gave students a booklet with four short stories or vignettes about staff interaction at a local newspaper. They asked the students to imagine being part of the situations. The students read the four vignettes and wrote their responses in the booklet.

Since the researchers didn't want the students to suspect any connection between the sexism survey and the stories in the booklet, the first and third vignettes were just fillers. The second vignette was the crucial one. There were three different booklets, but the only difference in the booklets was the second vignette. One-third of the participants got a booklet with a vignette containing nonsexist jokes. Here is an example of one of the nonsexist jokes: "What's the difference between a golfer and a skydiver? A golfer goes

---

1. See Ford et al., "More Than 'Just a Joke.'" Thomas Ford, working with other researchers, has done additional investigations that elaborate on the implications of sexist humor. See Ford et al., "Sexist Humor as a Trigger," and Ford et al., "Disparagement Humor and Prejudice."

whack . . . 'Damn!' A skydiver goes 'Damn! . . . whack.'" Another third of the participants got a booklet with a vignette containing sexist statements. Here's an example of one of these sexist statements: "I just think that a woman's place is in the home and that it's a woman's role to do domestic duties such as laundry for her man." The last third of participants got a booklet with a vignette containing sexist jokes. One of the sexist jokes was the joke I used to begin this chapter, the joke about the man and woman stranded in the elevator with the man making her "feel like a woman" by folding his laundry.

The second vignette was the variable. Some students read nonsexist jokes, some read sexist statements, and the last third read sexist jokes. The fourth vignette from the booklet gave participants a chance to respond. For this vignette, participants were told about a fictitious group called the National Council of Women. They were told that this council promoted political and social advancement for women, and that the council was seeking donations. The participants were then asked to imagine that they were working with the newspaper group. They were told to report how much they would donate to the National Council of Women, and they were told that they could donate anywhere between $20 and $0.

What the researchers found was that of participants who read the neutral jokes, those who were low or high in the hostile sexism survey scale donated about the same amount. For participants who read the sexist statements, again, there was little difference in their donations. But for the participants who read the sexist jokes, there was a significant difference. The participants who scored low on the hostile sexism survey gave the largest donation after reading the sexist jokes. In contrast, those who scored high on the hostile sexism survey donated much, much less money to the woman's organization. The nonsexist jokes and even the sexist statements didn't have an impact on donation. Sexist jokes did.

When the researchers considered these results, they concluded that the sexist participants got a different message from the sexist jokes than from the sexist statements. The statements may have reflected the ideas of sexist participants, but the ideas in themselves didn't impact behavior. It was the jokes that impacted behavior. Ford, Boxer, Armstrong, and Edel concluded that humor had the power to tell sexist participants that prejudiced attitudes didn't need to be taken too seriously. The jokes told prejudiced participants that other people shared their prejudiced views. You can imagine people like our imaginary Ryan and Dan saying that the elevator joke was just a joke. But at the same time, Ryan and Dan may get another message from the joke—that they are not the only ones who think that women don't need or deserve as much merit pay as men.

How Much Would You Cut?

Ford, Boxer, Armstrong, and Edel noted some limitations with their experiment. For one thing, participants wrote about what they imagined they might do. The experiment examines hypothetical behavior. In addition, the experiment didn't give a clear sense of how the jokes might lead to behavior. So the researchers set up a second experiment. Like the first, they started with the Ambivalent Sexism Inventory disguised as a Social Attitudes Survey. Again they gave students a two-week buffer. Then they explained that they were examining men's and women's responses to comedy videos, and that since they were looking at genders separately, they'd be working with only the men for now.

When the men arrived at the laboratory, they were told that they would respond to two brief studies. For the first study, researchers told the men that next year researchers would be using a series of comedic video clips. They wanted students to rate how funny the clips were. The students watched five clips, with half of the students watching four clips with sexist humor with a neutral clip thrown in to reduce suspicion. The clips played on sexist stereotypes like women as mere sex objects, women as raging feminists, and women as servants of their husbands. The other half of the students watched five nonsexist clips. Researchers asked the students to rate how funny the clips were, but this was not the real focus of the experiment.

After watching the clips, researchers asked participants to respond to another brief survey. This survey was about funding for student organizations. Researchers told the participants that next year's funding for student organizations was going to be cut by 20 percent. The five student organizations had nearly identical budgets, and each organization said that their current budget met their minimum needs. Each organization said that cuts would limit what the group could do and might even make it impossible for the organization to function. Researchers made the organizations sound like real university student organizations: Jewish Cultural Collective, Safe Arrival for Everyone, National Student Council for Women, Study Abroad Learning Program, and Michigan Black Student Union. Each participant had to decide how much to cut from each organization's budget. But researchers also asked the participants another important question: Did they think others would agree with their cuts? Participants used a seven-point scale to show if they thought the people in their immediate group would agree with their cuts.

Here again the results were remarkable. For those who watched the neutral clips, researchers didn't find any difference in how much the low or high sexist participants cut from the woman's organization. All participants cut the women's organization by about 20 percent, which is roughly the same as cuts to all five organization. It was a very different case for the participants who watched the sexist comedic video clips. Participants who scored high on the Ambivalent Sexism Inventory and who watched the sexist video clips cut funding by almost 30 percent. Here again, laughter released sexist attitudes and led to sexist behavior.

This left open the second question: Did the participants believe that others would agree with them? For this, researchers looked at the second part of the question. What they found was that participants who are high in hostile sexism believed that those in their immediate group agreed with them. In fact, those participants believed that their group agreed with them about cutting the women's organization, but they did not believe that their group would necessarily agree with them about cutting the other organizations. In other words, men who were high in the hostile sexism scale believed that their immediate group tolerated sexism. The participants who went to the study with hostile sexist beliefs, who saw the sexist comedic video clips, and who then cut the allocation to the university women's organization by 30 percent, believed that the other people in their group would have done the same thing.

The second experiment brings us back to Ryan. If Dan had simply told Ryan a joke, this research predicts that there would be no impact on Ryan's merit pay decisions. Even if Dan had said something overly sexist, like complaining about women in the company who should be having babies and doing housework, the research again predicts no impact. But if Dan signals his acceptance of sexist beliefs with a joke, this would have an impact. If Ryan already had hostile sexist attitudes, then this research predicts that Ryan might very well experience a release of those beliefs. Ryan may be completely unaware of how Dan's joke releases those attitudes. He may just brush it off as a joke. Ryan may feel confident that his decisions are fair and unbiased, claiming that, just as the research predicts, women in the company just deserve 10 percent less merit pay than the men. A sexist statement may not impact the sexist Ryans of the world, but a joke will.

CHAPTER 3

The Case of Kim Davis

IN HER MUGSHOT, YOU can see that she is five feet, five inches tall. She looks directly at the camera, and her mouth is a straight line under serious and determined eyes. You might view her determination as that of a bigoted woman using her interpretation of her religion and the First Amendment to do something ugly and hateful. You might view her determination as that of a brave woman of faith. She is humbly subservient to God in spite of the fact that her faith is about to land her in jail. There is another way that you might see her, but we'll get to that in a minute.

The woman is Rowan County clerk Kim Davis. On June 26, 2015, Davis had been at her job for about six months when the US Supreme Court made same-sex marriage in the United States legal. Davis, a devout Christian, was opposed to same-sex marriage. Rather than discriminate against same-sex couples, Davis decided that her office would not issue marriage licenses to anyone. After a local couple came to get a marriage license and Davis refused, the couple's video of the encounter went viral. Davis's face became the face of opposition to same-sex marriage.[1] The news that the woman defending marriage had been married four times and had had children out of wedlock made many see her as a hypocritical bigot. Others believed Davis when she affirmed that she was a flawed yet forgiven Christian who was acting according to the dictates of her conscience.

---

1. See Davis et al., *Under God's Authority*.

Insert Something Funny Here

What this next part of the chapter should include would be the best jokes about Davis. I could mention the opening song that Miley Cyrus sang in season forty-one of *Saturday Night Live*. Cyrus sang a version of "My Way."[2] While she sang, different actors from the show impersonated infamous news characters from the summer. They impersonated Rachel Dolezal, a white woman who passed for black; Jared Fogle, a disgraced Subway pitchman; and the dentist who killed the beloved Cecil the lion. They also impersonated Kim Davis. The Kim Davis impersonation shows her wearing the same outfit as in the mugshot. During the song, they impersonate Davis's exuberant "Praise the Lord" gesture she showed when she was released from jail. But Davis only had a bit part during this song, and it isn't particularly clever.

I could use a joke Andy Samberg told at the 2015 Emmy Awards. The first part of the joke was about Paula Deen, the famous Southern chef. Deen was in the news at the time because of racist statements she had made in the past. Around that same time, Deen was slated to be on *Dancing with the Stars*. Samberg's joke goes like this: "Paula Deen is on this season of *Dancing with the Stars*, but I've got to say, if I wanted to see an intolerant lady dance, I would have gone to one of Kim Davis's four weddings."[3] This joke is also not all that funny.

I could use some jokes from an opening monologue from *The Nightly Show with Larry Wilmore*.[4] I could mention how he jokingly compares Davis to Hitler, Jeffrey Dahmer, and George Wallace. He compares Davis's supporters to a lynch mob. Or I could describe the two videos sponsored by *Funny or Die*. One video connects news clips of Kim Davis with clips from *Parks and Recreation*.[5] The clips use some of Ron Swanson's statements to describe how evil Davis is. The other video mocks Davis's private meeting with Pope Francis.[6] This video makes her look ugly, stupid, and fanatical in her hatred of gays. Unfortunately, the opening monologue and videos are even less funny than the jokes already mentioned.

---

2. See Cyrus, "My Way."
3. See Horvitz, *Sixty-Seventh Primetime Emmy Awards Show,* 8:50–9:00.
4. See Allen, *Nightly Show with Larry Wilmore.*
5. See *Funny or Die*, "Clerks and Recreation."
6. See *Funny or Die*, "Kim Davis Met the Pope."

I spent hours searching for something really clever about Kim Davis. I wanted something that did more than take easy pot shots at her appearance and her working in Kentucky. I hoped to find something that might get into some of the situation's odd and potentially humorous contradictions. I hoped I might find something that touched on the fact that Davis got a lot of criticism from the political left and got support from many politicians on the right, while she herself was a lifelong, committed Democrat. I thought I might find something that got into the thorny First Amendment issues. It seemed like something clever could be made of how the ACLU chose to defend same-sex marriage rights but not for the right to find reasonable accommodations for someone's religious convictions.

I hoped to find something that played on other tensions. I hoped there would be something clever and funny comparing Davis to George Wallace or that compared Davis with Christian nurses who do not participate in abortions. The connection with George Wallace is that Wallace defied the federal government when he tried to stop mandatory school desegregation in Alabama. Many people critical of Davis made this connection. Those who defended Davis mentioned Christian nurses should not be required by their job to participate in something they find to be morally wrong. Davis believed she was making a very important moral decision. She said it was about heaven or hell. For her, signing same-sex marriage licenses would be consenting to, if not actively supporting, something she believed God thought was wrong. She believed God would punish her for doing such a thing. People opposed to Davis believed she was just the most recent bigot, not standing in front of the school but standing behind a desk, denying the rights and full citizenship of people who had been bullied, victimized, and oppressed. Perhaps it is just too difficult to make something funny that also insightfully explores different issues. But creating something funny and insightful seems to be part of comedy's job description. Maybe it is too much to ask, and that is why I never found it.

Smug Liberal Laughter

What inspired me to look up Davis and humorous responses to the news surrounding her was an article by Emmett Rensin. Rensin, whose article appeared in *Vox* in April 2016, is a writer and activist from the left side of the political spectrum. *Vox* is also liberal. One might expect that Rensin's article in *Vox* would criticize Kim Davis. What the article does is quite different.

Rensin's vigorous writing does not criticize the right, Kim Davis, or her supporters. Rensin criticizes American liberalism's smug style. His argument is that originally liberalism was about helping the poor and the powerless. Liberalism was unions struggling for better working conditions and pay. Liberalism was the New Deal—the liberal response to the Great Depression. It was bringing back all of the cards of wealth and power and then redistributing them, or redealing them, to achieve greater equality. Rensin puts forward that over time a gap formed between liberals and the people they were trying to help. Rensin notes that "by the 1990s the better part of the working class wanted nothing to do with the word *liberal*."[7] Perhaps your own experience might verify if working-class people have positive or negative attitudes toward that word. Rensin's focus is not why people developed negative ideas about liberalism in the past. His focus is on why people have negative views now. In other words, why would the very people that liberals want to help be so turned off by liberals? Oh, and one more thing—Rensin is speaking to liberals themselves. He is not trying to convince working-class people that liberals really do want to make life better for them. He is trying to explain to liberals why such people need convincing at all. Rensin's article is not a deep, complex, philosophical essay. It is not a historical analysis. It is not a social science or political science article written in an academic style. It is a lively, biting criticism of liberals.

Smugness—that is what Rensin really criticizes. Liberal smugness is what divides liberals from those they aim to help. This smugness comes out in how liberals look down on working-class people. Liberals end up seeing working-class people as too foolish to know what is good for them. These condescending attitudes dominate liberal shows and entertainment. As Rensin puts it, the condescending attitudes "began in humor, and culminated for a time in *The Daily Show*."[8] What Rensin sees in programs like *The Daily Show* is a slick and clever program that celebrates how cool liberals and their ideas are. The show ridicules liberal opponents as stupid and uncool. Rensin puts forward that smug liberals enjoy shows like this because they flatter their ideas and ridicule the uncool who do not see things as they do.

When Rensin provides an example of the stupid and the uncool, the people and ideas that liberals ridicule, his example is Kim Davis. Rensin says, "Dour, rural, thrice divorced but born again—Twitter could not have

---

7. Rensin, "Smug Style in American Liberalism," para. 10 (italics original).
8. Rensin, "Smug Style in American Liberalism," para. 16.

invented a better parody of the uncool."[9] But that is not all the liberals ridiculed. Rensin says that what liberals saw in Davis was someone who was "a hateful bigot who did not even understand her own religion."[10] Davis is wrong because she does not understand Christianity the way that the cool liberals understand it. Rensin says that this is the conclusion liberals draw: "there are no moral fights" since those who don't believe as liberals do are either "lying liars or the stupid rubes who believe them."[11] Davis and her supporters are probably in the second group, stupid rubes, while conservative politicians and leaders are the lying liars.

What Rensin sees in smug liberal laughter, laughter found in left-leaning shows like *Saturday Night Live* and *The Nightly Show with Larry Wilmore*, on left-leaning YouTube channels like *Funny or Die* and on left-dominated entertainment industries and award shows like the Emmys, is actually much deeper than just elitist ridicule. Smug liberal laughter is more than just cultural elites mocking those they claim to want to help. Smug liberal laughter is a "failure of empathy."[12] Liberals are unwilling to vulnerably connect with those who see and believe differently than they do. They are unwilling to do the difficult work of genuinely listening to them. They cannot respectfully enter into conversations with them. What liberals do is insist that others get on board with their ideas, dismiss them as too stupid if they don't, or else liberals hit them over the head with facts and jokes as if such assaults will bring them to their senses. But for Rensin it is impossible to separate a desire to help people from your "duty to respect them."[13]

Smug Conservative Laughter

What this chapter should end with is an example from the right side of the political spectrum. It should give a clever example or two of how smug conservatives look down on liberals. It could be something funny about liberal "snowflakes" or about fanatical "social justice warriors." It could be a witty criticism of "feminazis" or "antifa" nutjobs or even just "libtards" in general. Such things probably exist, but there is also a good chance that they don't. I did a lot of looking, and I never found them. The truth is that the culture

9. Rensin, "Smug Style in American Liberalism," para. 38.
10. Rensin, "Smug Style in American Liberalism," para. 42.
11. Rensin, "Smug Style in American Liberalism," para. 47.
12. Rensin, "Smug Style in American Liberalism," para. 137.
13. Rensin, "Smug Style in American Liberalism," para. 134.

one sees in the early twenty-first century in the United States does not have a right-leaning equivalent to *Saturday Night Live* or *The Daily Show*. This does not mean that conservatives don't look down on liberals. The insults given at the beginning of this paragraph are common conservative insults for those who disagree with them. Conservatives can have a parallel lack of empathy. While conservatives do not control the humor means of production that liberals have, they have very popular political commentators to do that smug and disrespectful work.

Liberal and conservative smugness and disrespect force a false choice. People like Kim Davis are either hateful bigots who fundamentally misunderstand their religion, picking and choosing what they like and defying the government and the rule of law, or they are valiant heroes defending their faith and the rights guaranteed to them by the Constitution. Kim Davis is either the reincarnated George Wallace, barring loving couples from marriage, or she is George Daniel Washington, crossing the Delaware on his way to the lion's den. When we reject smug laughter and its lack of empathy, what we find in Kim Davis are the complexities, flaws, and struggles to live up to one's principles. In this, Kim Davis turns out to be like all of us. Sadly, smug laughter makes it impossible to witness and embrace the humanity we share with others. It might even blind us to our own humanity.

CHAPTER 4

A Frenchman, a Spaniard, an American, and an Onion

A FRENCHMAN HUMS TO himself while he paints in his Paris studio. His calm exterior hides two intense competitions. The painter, Georges Braque, is competing with his close friend, the Spanish painter Pablo Picasso. Many years after this moment, Braque will compare his relationship with Picasso to two mountain climbers.[1] Braque imagines that one climber scales up the mountain past his companion and then the second climber uses his partner's height and leverage to climb even higher. Both painters get to the top of the mountain, or reach artistic heights, by learning from and then outdoing the other. At this moment in 1911, Braque wants to outdo Picasso.

Braque's second competition is with the Louvre. In fact, these friends have a little saying: some paintings are the Louvre, and some are Dufayel.[2] Dufayel was a department store, a place well known at the time from its advertising that was pasted all over Paris. What this saying meant is that a painting could look like traditional art, like something in the Louvre, or it could look like something commercial and popular. But Dufayel wasn't just popular and commercial. This department store was in a working-class neighborhood. Dufayel was not Barney's, Bloomingdale's, or Saks Fifth Avenue; Dufayel was Walmart. When Braque and Picasso would visit each

1. Friedenthal, *Letters of the Great Artists*, 264.
2. Danchev, *Georges Braque*, 69. For more information about Dufayel see Wemp "Social Space."

other's Parisian studios, which they did almost daily, they would look at each other's paintings and comment, "Nope, that's still the Louvre." A better painting would be at least a little bit Dufayel.

What do Braque and Picasso mean by this distinction? A good example of a painting that is literally in the Louvre is the portrait of Mademoiselle Caroline Rivière (figure 1).[3]

Figure 1. Ingres, Jean Auguste Dominique. 1805. *Mademoiselle Riviere.*
Paris, Musée du Louvre. Photo Credit: Scala / Art Resource, NY.

Caroline is the teenage daughter of wealthy, successful parents. She wears a lovely white dress tied high on her waist. A white fur boa is draped over her forearm, and the rest of that arm is covered with elegant tan gloves. The white boa matches her fair neck and face. She has a bit of red in the lips and cheeks, and the painting's white and red are set off by her deep black hair and dark eyes. Caroline is quite close to the viewer. The portrait gives us a three-quarters view of her. Deep in the background, water reflects

3. See Siegfried, *Ingres*, 94–95.

the blue of the sky. Among the green trees and foliage is a similarly blue church steeple. The artist, Jean Auguste Dominique Ingres, shows off his tremendous skills in the lovely figure, in the variety of textures, in the use of white, red, and black, and in details like the intricately drawn gloves and sleeve. The painter does his work with such skill that it does not look like paint on a flat surface. It looks like there is a lovely woman right there. The painting begs you to strike up a conversation with her or at least reach out and touch her fur boa.

Braque's Cluttered and Crafty Painting of *The Portuguese*

Braque and Picasso reject paintings like this. Braque, as he hums to himself in his studio in 1911, is painting a portrait. His work is called *The Portuguese* (figure 2).

Figure 2. Braque, Georges. 1911. *The Portuguese*. Basel, Kunstmuseum.

This portrait is difficult to figure out. Toward the lower center is most of a circle cut by four horizontal lines. This circle seems to be a guitar's sound hole with strings over it. The diagonal coming up from the sound hole could be the instrument's fretboard and neck. If that is the neck, then we could make out a shoulder and arm on the right side, and maybe fingers. On the other side we could see the diagonal of an arm and horizontal forearm holding the guitar. Where we would expect a face to be we could guess at a smile or the closed eyes of someone singing while playing, but it is difficult to make out. There is a white patch, and at the top of that patch are curved lines like a smile. There is also a white patch at the center of the very top of the painting. To the right of what should be the person is something that looks like a bottle, something else that looks like rope, and something that might be a post, perhaps on a pier. To the left is something that looks like a pulley. Braque stenciled the letters "DBAL" right onto the picture, below them an "&," and below that an "N" or "M" followed by "0,40." On the other side he stenciled part of "D" or an "O," followed by "CO." If this painting is funny or if it is about everyday things instead of fine art, then it seems like the joke is on us.

Braque's portrait is quite different from Ingres's Louvre portrait. In Braque's painting the figure is difficult to even identify. We can perhaps make out parts, as we have attempted to do, but the person is difficult to see. The space around the figure is also confusing. That space, instead of being empty, seems to be cluttered and even alive. Maybe Braque's musician is playing and moving. Is that why the figure is hard to see clearly? Is that what makes the space around the figure blurry as well? And speaking of the space, one possibility is that the pulley to the left and the rope on the right of the figure could be some sort of curtain. Perhaps the person is on a stage with a curtain that can be raised or lowered. The curtain could be pulled back and hitched, but the figure is still difficult to make out. Ingres and the Louvre offer an easy-to-see figure in a normal space, while Braque's swaying or grooving musician is as difficult to pin down as the objects and the cluttered space surrounding it.

There might even be more going on with the space in Braque's painting. What if we see the rope to the right as attached to a pier? If that is the case, then the white shape over the figure might be a cloud and the figure is outside like Caroline Rivière. But if the pulley and rope are part of curtains over a window, then the person is inside. In Braque's filled, cluttered, and confusing space, we can't even tell if the figure is inside or outside.

There is one more thing that makes the space even harder to figure out—the stenciled letters. Are those letters supposed to be on signs in the background? Is this some sort of bar or dance hall? If that is the case, then the numbers might be prices posted on the walls. In fact, "D BAL" might be part of the words "[GRAN]D BAL," as in a "Grand Ball" or large, elegant dance and social gathering space. But the letters don't seem to be in the background like we expect. They are not in a deep space, nor are they at an angle on a wall. The letters don't seem hazy like letters that are far away. Instead, Braque stenciled the letters right onto the picture. Those letters remind us that the painting is a painting, something flat with paint and stenciled letters on it.

What might the vague, hard-to-identify person and the confusing space in this painting have to do with the Louvre and Dufayel? Those elements relate to the Louvre because Braque is playing with all of the normal qualities we would expect from portraits we would see in the Louvre like Ingres's portrait of Mademoiselle Caroline Rivière. Instead of a clear figure, we have one that is ambiguous. Instead of an easy-to-understand location, we have difficulty figuring out if the person is inside or outside. Instead of empty space, the area around the figure is filled and cluttered. Instead of the illusion of a person in a three-dimensional area, we have those letters that keep reminding us that this is actually a two-dimensional picture.

So what is Dufayel about Braque's work? While the above elements are different from what we'd find in a fine art museum, Braque's use of stencils is definitely closer to Dufayel than the Louvre. In fact, part of what is so interesting about this painting is Braque's use of stencils. In previous works, he and Picasso had put letters in paintings, but those letters had been drawn and painted. This painting was the first time either artist had used stencils. Even today, stencils are craft items you can find in Walmart. Stenciling is not a skill you learn in prestigious painting academies. Both Picasso and Braque had been trained in academies to produce fine art for places like the Louvre, but Braque had also learned a different set of skills from his father. Braque's father was a painter-decorator, a man who would be hired to paint things like billboards or signs for a shop. Painter-decorators used things like stencils to make posters, billboards, signs, or even advertising for places like Dufayel. Using stencils, a very common and popular tool, is one important way that *The Portuguese* leans toward Dufayel and away from the Louvre.

But Braque has a few more jokes in this painting, jokes that go against the seriousness we might expect from traditional portraits. One very well-known book of the time, a book that all French public-school children would have read, is a story about an affair between a French soldier and a nun. The nun has a portrait of the soldier that she looks at constantly. She talks about him sailing away. She is stuck in a confined space that she longs to leave. Oh, and the nun is Portuguese, and the book is called *The Portuguese Letters*. Braque's painting *The Portuguese* features stenciled letters. And yes, just like in English, *lettre* in French can mean mailed correspondence or letters in the alphabet.[4]

The connection between Braque's painting with stenciled letters called *The Portuguese* and the popular French schoolbook *The Portuguese Letters* could just be a coincidence. But it turns out that there are other connections. As noted, the space in Braque's painting is difficult to understand. The painting could be a portrait of someone inside, perhaps a nun in the convent thinking of her departed lover. It might be the nun dreaming about the pier and the lover sailing away with a cloud overhead. The white portion under the mouth could be a white bib, part of a nun's headdress or wimple. Seen in this way, the vague white patch on top of the figure could be another part of the nun's headdress. Nun or musician, someone inside a cloister, on a pier, in a café or dance hall—this painting plays with all of those possibilities. In playing with all of those possibilities, *The Portuguese* is a fun, ambiguous, and crafty painting that celebrates Dufayel and makes fun of the Louvre and its refined seriousness.

Maybe it still seems like a stretch to say that this hard-to-understand portrait by Georges Braque that has letters and is called *The Portuguese* is a visual game about *The Portuguese Letters*. Two more bits of evidence support this idea—Picasso and Braque's statements about the playfulness of their work and a few more visual and verbal jokes in this painting.

Speaking many years later, Braque mentioned that he rejected traditional perspective. He rejected the traditional ways that painters give the illusion of a three-dimensional space on a two-dimensional surface. Braque also embraced a new approach to space, wanting to make space into something you could touch. He went so far as to say that it was "space that attracted me strongly" and that paintings of this time were "the quest

4. See Cloonan, "Braque's *Le Portugais*."

for space."[5] Braque's ideas, and paintings like this one, show a very different approach to space than traditional portraits.

In addition to talking about space, Braque also spoke about the conversations he used to have with Picasso. For Braque, these conversations were very unique. Braque said that "things were said with Picasso during those years that no one will ever say again, things that no one could ever say any more."[6] Braque elaborates that those things were "things that would be incomprehensible [to others] and which gave us such great joy."[7] Braque and Picasso's friend of the time, André Salmon, said that he and the artists of their circle "made continual fun of everything" and they "invented an artificial world with countless jokes that were quite unintelligible to others."[8] Statements like these support the idea that Braque and Picasso used visual and verbal puns in their everyday lives and in their work, puns that made fun of virtually everything around them.

And there are at least two more puns in Braque's painting. The stenciled letters "D BAL" could be part of the phrase "Grand Bal," as already mentioned. They could also be a play on the French word *déballe*, which means "unpack." In a painting about letters, stamps, and perhaps packages, this pun invites us to unpack the different parts, possibilities, and meanings. And then there are the letters "OCO" on the other side. Those letters happen to spell out the Portuguese word for "hollow." Right when the lettering invites us to unpack the painting, it humorously warns us that the painting, the letters, and the entire search might be hollow or empty. It is also humorous to note that these letters for hollow are stamped on a painting that is anything but hollow; it is cluttered and filled with space you can almost touch. We cannot know if this is an accurate unpacking of Braque's painting. The artist was quite right when he warned how difficult it would be for others to understand the many inside jokes that this group shared.

Picasso Outclimbs Braque with "Our Victory Is in the Air"

We can guess that Braque was pleased with his Dufayel response to the Louvre and to traditional portraits. He may have felt, quite rightly, that he

---

5. Friedenthal, *Letters of the Great Artists*, 264.

6. Danchev, *Georges Braque*, 60.

7. Danchev, *Georges Braque*, 60.

8. See Cloonan, "Braque's *Le Portugais*," 607.

had climbed above and ahead of Picasso. So now it was Picasso's turn to learn from and to outdo Braque.

And it didn't take long for Picasso to respond to Braque. In May 1912, Picasso painted a still life called *The Scallop Shell: "Notre Avenir est dans l'air"* (figure 3).

Figure 3. Picasso, Pablo. 1912. *The Scallop Shell: "Notre Avenir est dans l'air."* New York, Metropolitan Museum of Art. Promised Gift from the Leonard A. Lauder Cubist Collection. © Estate of Pablo Picasso / Artists Rights Society (ARS), New York. Art Resource, NY.

What we see in Picasso's painting are many of the same things we saw in Braque's. The painting has a lot of browns, pale yellows, and white. It also has a confusing space and objects that are hard to make out. Toward the center of the painting are two white shapes that seem to be the title's scallop shells. Above them are black lines that might define a third shell. Right above that shell are two curved lines that might make the profile of a glass. These items give us the sense that we have a table with several scallop shells and a glass. To the left of the glass is what looks like a pipe. The pipe seems to be sitting on a popular brochure of the time. The title of the red-white-and-blue brochure could be translated as "Our Victory Is in the Air." To the far left of the painting is a rectangular space with the letters "JOU." Those are the first three letters of the French word for "newspaper" or "journal."

Taken together, what we have is an oval-shaped still life of a table upon which we find scallop shells, a glass, a pipe, a brochure, and a newspaper. How does this painting show Picasso climbing up and catching up with his friend Braque but then going past him? And how might this painting be more Dufayel than even Braque's portrait?

The space in Picasso's still life is just as cluttered and unclear as the space in Braque's portrait. The newspaper or journal does not lie flat and recede into space. And the angle for the brochure is really wrong. It's at an angle, but it doesn't seem to go back in space. There are diagonal lines in the brochure, as well as the diagonal line behind the newspaper, but none of those lines add up to objects moving back in a three-dimensional space. Picasso, like Braque, plays with space. But Picasso includes a very clever little joke about their shared interest in space with the brochure's title: "Our Victory Is in the Air." On one level, victory is in the air, or just about to happen. But another way that victory is in the air is how the painting is about conquering the air, or rethinking how air and space are depicted in paintings. Another victory could be Picasso's victory over traditional art, over the Louvre, and even over Braque.

But there is another way that this part of the painting is Dufayel beating out the Louvre. The very paint that Picasso uses here is not regular artist paint. Picasso is painting with ripolin, which was paint that a painter-decorator would use.[9] It is as if Picasso went to Sherman Williams to pick up paint for this still life. This is just one more example of these two artists choosing the commercial and the popular over the traditional.

Besides the joke with the brochure about victory in the air or in the space in these paintings, Picasso is also creating a whole host of puns from the letters on the left side. As mentioned previously, "JOU" are the first letters of the French word for newspaper or journal. We could see this as a newspaper covered by something or folded so we only see these letters. But "JOU" are also the first letters of several French words that could create delightful puns.[10] The French word *Jouer* means to play or to fool, and *joujou* is a toy or plaything. Picasso is playing with the seriousness of traditional art and the traditional ways that still lifes are done. *Jouailler* means to play a musical instrument poorly. This could be another inside joke, since Picasso could not even read music while Braque was an accomplished musician. Finally, *jouansse* means the kick or thrill of drugs, *jouissance* is a word for

9. See Richardson and McCully, *Life of Picasso*, 225.
10. See Frascina, "Realism and Ideology," 156–57.

orgasm, and *jouir* is a verb meaning to have an orgasm. Clearly this painting includes many possibilities for verbal and visual jokes.

There is one more element of this painting to mention, one more way that it would have been funny to the artists and their circle. The brochure *Notre Avenir est dans l'Air* presents military arguments for the development of airplanes as tools and weapons. In fact, airplanes were all the rage at this time, so much so that one of Picasso's nicknames for Braque was Wilbourg, after Wilbur Wright.[11] Picasso and Braque thought of themselves as the Wright brothers, and they found victory in the air—victory about to happen and victory in their approach to space—in their competition with traditional art. Picasso's still life may have moved up and past Braque, being even more clever and more Dufayel, but the battle, the climbing, and the competitions, would continue.

An American Paints Back and an Onion

Picasso's still life and Braque's portrait are funny, clever, and crafty, at least to them. With that, we can look at one last painting: Mark Tansey's painting *Picasso and Braque* (figure 4). Tansey is an American artist, and his 1992 painting shows Picasso and Braque as the Wright brothers. Tansey anticipates that you know about Picasso's nickname for Braque and their fascination with the Wright brothers. He also anticipates that you know about the art that they created together. Part of what is so funny and clever about the painting is how the airplane that Picasso is flying is made up of lines, patches, and shapes that use the visual style of paintings like *The Portuguese, The Scallop Shell: "Nortre Avenir est dans l'air,"* and similar works by these artists. Tansey's work is funny and clever, though in ways that are different from Picasso and Braque's work.

So why, in a book that is supposed to explore if laughter can make the world a better place, and in a section called "No," would there be this discussion of paintings made over 100 years ago by a Frenchman and by a Spaniard, with an additional painting made much more recently by an American? Before exploring that connection, let me admit that some of you might not have found Tansey or Picasso or Braque's paintings very funny. You might not see them as clever, witty, or crafty. So let me try again. This time I will use witty and clever examples from *The Onion*, a satirical newspaper that is also available online.

11. See Danchev, *Georges Braque*, 68.

Figure 4. Tansey, Mark. 1992. *Picasso and Braque.* **Los Angeles, LA County Museum of Art. © Mark Tansey. Used by permission of the artist.**

In June 1998, *The Onion* published an article with the following title: "New Starbucks Opens in Rest Room of Existing Starbucks."[12] In December 2007 they published a photo of a large plastic ball in a far corner of an apartment with the caption, "Exercise Ball All The Way Over There."[13] A headline from June 2001 reads, "Nobel Fever Grips Research Community as Prize Swells to $190 Million."[14]

What is the common element in these *Onion* headlines, in Mark Tansey's painting of Picasso and Braque, and in Braque and Picasso's paintings? All of these might cause you to laugh in a light and delightful manner. They could bring surprise, fun, and mirth. So why are they in the "No" section? They are in the No section because making the world a better place is not laughter's job. Laughter is a pleasing surprise, delightful fun, and mirthful response. It can come by noticing visual and verbal puns. It can come by seeing how someone plays with our expectations. It can come when we

12. "New Starbucks Opens."
13. "Exercise Ball."
14. "Nobel Fever Grips Research Community."

find delight in a humorous comparison between the Nobel prize and the lottery or when someone points out how absurd it is that there are so many Starbucks. To ask laughter to be more than that, to ask it to change or transform the world in some grand and monumental way, is out of place, if not ridiculous. Changing the world just isn't laughter's job.

Allowing laughter's delight to be just delight eliminates the need for it to change the world. That might be the best, or at least the least-damaging, version of laughter in this section. When laughter does change the world, it makes it worse. Laughter is smug liberals or conservatives making fun of people who see things differently. Smug laughter eliminates empathy, severs connections, and deepens divisions. Or laughter brings out the worst in people. People who already have ugly, bigoted opinions of others can share those opinions under the cover of "it's just a joke." The joke invites people to take their biased attitudes less seriously, and the joke releases socially unacceptable attitudes. Jokes make those ugly attitudes seem commonplace and shared. This sort of laughter is a subtle but powerful weapon that can have real-world consequences. Laughter in a bully's hands is a particularly terrible tool. That laughter creates hostile and coercive work and home environments. Such laughter gives people power to do terrible, abusive things. In homes, at work, in hospitals, in groups large and small, in families, marriages, and individual lives, this laughter damages everything it touches.

Maybe

CHAPTER 5

Malcolm and a Dead Russian Go to Burning Man

THE OLDER OF THE two teenage brothers is keeping an eye out for their parents. The other brother is kneeling on the bathroom floor, writing a note on the toilet paper. That younger brother, Malcolm, unrolls the tissue and guesses how much each family member will use. He unrolls about eight squares for one sibling, eight more for another, and then about thirty-four for his dad. Once he gets well into the roll, he writes a message—he and his brother Reese have gone to Burning Man. Malcolm rolls the toilet paper back up, leaving both brothers confident that they will now have plenty of time to hitchhike to the annual festival in Black Rock City, Nevada.

The scene cuts immediately to their parents dragging them into the house. Their angry and frustrated mother, Lois, is yelling at them, "Hitchhiking?! Hitchhiking out on the highway like hobos?!"[1] An equally enraged father, Hal, says, "Thank God your mother undercooked the chicken last night or who knows when we might have found out about this!"[2]

Lois then asks her teenage sons a pivotal question. The first part of the question is one every parent of teenagers eventually asks—"What were you thinking"—but the rest of the question is rather unique—"sneaking off in the middle of the night to go to some overblown keg party in the desert?!"[3] For some reason, Malcolm sees this as an opening. His exasperated mother wants to know why, and Malcolm says that Burning Man is not what she thinks it is. Full of passion, he says, "Burning Man is an incredible,

---

1. Lauer, *Malcolm in the Middle*, 1:55.
2. Lauer, *Malcolm in the Middle*, 1:57–2:01.
3. Lauer, *Malcolm in the Middle*, 2:07–2:08.

interactive experiment in human creativity, where you do art just for art's sake, and you make music from instruments that came to you in dreams."[4] Sensing that his parents are listening, Malcolm continues, "It's the one place where you're free to let go and really see what you're capable of creating without worrying what anyone else thinks! That's what Burning Man is all about!"[5] There is a pause. Lois and Hal stand in stunned silence. Malcolm looks into the camera and confides in the viewers, "I think she actually might've bought that."[6]

These are some of the important first moments in "Burning Man," the first episode of the seventh season of the television show *Malcolm in the Middle*. The episode explores how each family member responds to the experimental community festival that is Burning Man. We could just watch this very funny episode, but instead we are going to metaphorically travel there with the family in the company of a dead Russian. Our dead Russian is Mikhail Bakhtin. It is doubtful that Bakhtin ever saw this particular television episode, mostly because he had been dead for thirty-two years when it first aired. Still, as we will see, some of Bakhtin's ideas provide vivid insights into how the family members respond to the experiment in human creativity and freedom that is Burning Man.

Hal and Reese

Hal, Lois, Reese, Malcolm, Dewey, and Jamie Wilkerson go to Burning Man in the RV Hal borrowed from his boss. Hal took his boss's RV because he did a noble deed for his boss—he took the blame for a fart in an elevator. That is how you win friends, influence people, and move up in the cutthroat business world of today. Hal is really looking forward to this vacation, but even so, he wants to make sure he can return his boss's RV without a stain, smudge, smell, or dent. Hal also seems to have a rather imperfect understanding of Burning Man. After parking the RV, he rolls out a green, artificial turf carpet, notices the approaching festivalgoers, and promises to grill up for them the best burgers and dogs they have ever had. The festivalgoers, the people at Burning Man, are bewildered. As the episode goes on, more festivalgoers stop to observe Hal. Hal eventually comments to himself,

4. Lauer, *Malcolm in the Middle*, 2:12–2:19.
5. Lauer, *Malcolm in the Middle*, 2:20–2:30.
6. Lauer, *Malcolm in the Middle*, 2:33.

"Mention free food and they gather like flies."[7] Later in the episode, when Hal is sweeping some of the sand off of his artificial turf carpet, he wonders aloud to the onlookers, "What are you looking at?! Haven't you ever seen a man sweep his lawn with a broom before?"[8] No, they haven't. They haven't seen a man at Burning Man acting the way Hal is.

Hal does not really understand the principles behind Burning Man. Hal does not see it as Malcolm described. For Hal it is not a "place where you're free to let go and really see what you're capable of creating without worrying what anyone else thinks."[9] For Hal this is merely taking the family for a camping vacation in the desert. It is camping in the desert with a really nice RV. Some of the festivalgoers seem entranced by what Hal is doing. One confused onlooker asks another, "What's he doing?"[10] The second onlooker responds with a sly smile, "It's performance art. He's skewering the empty banality of the modern suburban dad."[11] The festivalgoers take what Hal is doing as sarcastic parody. One says to another, "This piece is as vicious as it is funny."[12] But while they see what Hal is doing as darkly humorous, Hal has no idea why they are staring at him. At one point in the show, right at a time when Hal's tired, confused, and frustrated with their staring, a Frisbee hits the side of the RV. Hal rushes to inspect the damage, worried that it may have left a mark. Grabbing the Frisbee and shaking it in his fist, Hal yells to the onlookers, "What the hell is wrong with you people?! Doesn't anybody have respect for personal property anymore? You can think about that for a few days until I give this back to you."[13] Hal's stereotypical angry-suburban-father punishment provokes loud and appreciative laughter from the onlookers. The onlookers are amused, and Hal, of course, is even more bewildered by their amusement.

At one point Hal tells Lois he really doesn't like this place. This is the exact opposite of his son Reese's opinion. When Reese first gets to Burning Man, his interests seems focused on the gratification of adolescent male sexual desire. He asks an older-looking gentleman where he can find the

---

7. Lauer, *Malcolm in the Middle*, 8:25–8:28.

8. Lauer, *Malcolm in the Middle*, 13:24–13:30.

9. Lauer, *Malcolm in the Middle*, 2:20–2:30.

10. Lauer, *Malcolm in the Middle*, 7:18.

11. Lauer, *Malcolm in the Middle*, 7:20–7:25.

12. Lauer, *Malcolm in the Middle*, 13:21–13:23.

13. Lauer, *Malcolm in the Middle*, 13:43–13:55.

attractive "topless chicks."[14] The man tells Reese that he is going that way, inviting the boy to follow. But this older man has a large squirt gun. It is more like a squirt rifle or a super soaker. This particular gun is not filled with water, as one would expect. As Burning Man community members approach the man, he says, "Want some Stanley?"[15] and then shoots them with grayish powder from the gun. After it happens more than once, Reese asks the man, "What's Stanley?"[16] The man explains that "Stanley" was a friend who accompanied him to Burning Man for many, many years. Stanley had died over the winter, but he wanted his ashes spread at Burning Man "to spread the spirit of Burning Man to the people and family he loved."[17] Reese is duly shocked that there is such a place where you can "spray a dead guy at people."[18] He says that he got a week of school suspension for something far less serious. The man explains that Burning Man is about freedom. It's a place to do whatever you want. He tells Reese that the real spirit of Burning Man is "about creating, participating, contributing, building a community that needs you, relies on you."[19] He elaborates that "it is allowing yourself to become part of the whole, and then coming away from it with more than you brought."[20] He finishes with, "It is a mind-altering journey, son, if you're willing to take it."[21] An enthralled Reese enthusiastically responds with a shake of the head, "You know what, I think I want some Stanley!"[22]

As Reese enjoys being soaked or doused with Stanley's ashes, he enters Burning Man's community and joins its mind-altering journey of freedom and self-discovery. Reese joins a group that might be the Men's Diaper Brigade, and, toward the end of the show, dances exuberantly around a fire. Reese's willingness to relish the spirit of Burning Man is even rewarded at the end. The man he had seen before tells Reese that because he has embraced and embodied the spirit of the festival, Reese will have the honor of wielding the torch that will burn "the Man." "The Man" in this case is the towering wooden effigy. At first, Reese is honored. But then, he realizes that

14. Lauer, *Malcolm in the Middle*, 5:14.
15. Lauer, *Malcolm in the Middle*, 5:23.
16. Lauer, *Malcolm in the Middle*, 5:33.
17. Lauer, *Malcolm in the Middle*, 5:48–5:53.
18. Lauer, *Malcolm in the Middle*, 5:55.
19. Lauer, *Malcolm in the Middle*, 6:28–6:35.
20. Lauer, *Malcolm in the Middle*, 6:35–6:40.
21. Lauer, *Malcolm in the Middle*, 6:44–6:49.
22. Lauer, *Malcolm in the Middle*, 6:53–6:54.

burning "the Man" will bring an end to the festival. Desperate, Reese says, "But it can't end! I don't want it to! For the first time in my life I feel real!"[23] When they try to take the torch from Reese, he threatens them. He says, "Everyone just stay back—no one's burning Burning Man!"[24]

Brief Disney Sidetrack

Hal and Reese have very different experiences at Burning Man. Bakhtin's ideas help us understand those differences. Bakhtin describes what I think is the true spirit of Burning Man, and in my dream world it is Bakhtin's ashes that are being spread at the festival. But before I explain how Bakhtin explains the carnival spirit of Burning Man, we have to talk about a Disney movie. That Disney movie is *The Hunchback of Notre Dame*. Toward the beginning of the movie, Quasimodo, the hunchback of Notre Dame, tells a small bird that today is a good day to fly away from the nest. Even children see the symbolism here. Quasimodo is confined to the cathedral. He does not dare to risk leaving. In part he is afraid of his master, Judge Frollo. But he is also afraid that he doesn't fit in among normal people. He's afraid he will be rejected. But just as Quasimodo had encouraged the small bird to fly away from the nest, he ends up deciding to leave the cathedral. In fact, Quasimodo has decided to go into the main city square adjacent to the cathedral and enjoy the Feast of Fools.

In the Disney film, the Feast of Fools is accompanied by the song "Topsy-Turvy."[25] The song begins with an invitation to set aside daily tasks and close the churches and schools. Those places are closed because this will be a time to break the rules. While breaking the rules is an important part of the feast, there is much more to it. The song is called "Topsy Turvy" because everything is turned upside down. The song describes how, during the Feast of Fools, common people and royalty temporarily switch places. The movie shows this with a man dressed as a king doing a flip so that his outfit changes from that of a king to that of a clown. The song and movie include reversals like these—gold becomes dross and weeds are a bouquet. Visual reversals in the movie include dogs holding leashes and taking men for walks and a lobster boiling a chef in a portable pot. We see a seductive Romani woman making fun of the city's most imposing judge. The

---

23. Lauer, *Malcolm in the Middle*, 17:31–17:34.
24. Lauer, *Malcolm in the Middle*, 17:47–17:48.
25. Menken and Schwartz, "Topsy-Turvey."

crowning event is literally a crowning. The king of the Feast of Fools is not a wise aristocrat with God-given power. He does not look noble and dignified. The king of the Feast of Fools is the festival's ugliest person. Various ugly men pull faces to win the prize, only to all be rejected. The last man standing is Quasimodo. When it turns out that he isn't wearing a mask, and that, instead, he's just that ugly, people initially recoil in dread. But this lasts only for a moment. Quasimodo is almost immediately received as a perfect king for the Feast of Fools.

The Feast of Fools is about turning things upside down. The social order is reversed, with a clown acting as master of ceremonies. The powerful judge is sidelined and powerless. The noble and the beautiful take a back seat to the grotesque and the hideous. The natural order is also reversed. Dogs walk humans and lobsters cook chefs. What is normally worthless— dross and weeds—become the most valuable and the highest prized. But besides these things that are turned upside down, there is also a suspension if not reversal of the moral order of things. The song says that the Feast of Fools is a time for the devil to run free and for people to do everything that is otherwise forbidden. Rules and social norms no longer apply. Finally, at the Feast of Fools, people not only break the rules, but they insult and shock religious and political authorities.

Okay, One More Sidetrack

I know that I said that I would use the Disney movie for my example, but I have one more very quick example. When I talk about Bakhtin's ideas in my college class, we have a discussion about the differences between a fraternity or sorority party and graduation. Most of my students don't see these things as similar at all. But what I tell them is that both are festivals or celebrations. A graduation is a festival that marks the completion of one's college degree. It is a very formal festival. People are carefully arranged by their rank and their status. University officials are up on stage, and graduates are evenly and orderly seated facing them. Around the outside are the family and friends who celebrate with the graduates. University officials are dressed in formal attire. Their clothing as well as other symbols demonstrate their authority. Graduates are also formally dressed. Mothers and fathers get dressed up for graduation, and even younger siblings are forced to wear formal and generally uncomfortable clothing. This is a very serious yet cheerful ceremony.

In the weeks and years before graduation, those same formally dressed graduates may have attended parties hosted by the school's fraternities or sororities. These are obviously very informal celebrations. Nothing in particular is being celebrated except for maybe it is a day ending in the letter "y." Nothing is carefully arranged, and generally there is no status or rank. There are no symbols of authority, mothers or fathers, nor anything very serious. There very well may be plenty of alcohol.

Bakhtin and the Carnival

I'm not sure if Bakhtin ever went to a wild fraternity or sorority party during his many years in Russian universities. I am sure he never saw Disney's *The Hunchback of Notre Dame* because he had been dead for twenty-three-years. But Bakhtin was an expert on medieval European culture and on the French Renaissance writer François Rabelais. What Bakhtin has to say about that culture and the writer reveal interesting things about graduation ceremonies, fraternity and sorority parties, and the Feast of Fools in *The Hunchback of Notre Dame*.

In the 1930s, Bakhtin wrote a book with the English title *Rabelais and His World*. To describe Rabelais's world and culture, Bakhtin talks about two different types of medieval festival. The first type of festival are official festivals. These are serious religious and political ceremonies like Christmas or Easter festivals or coronations. These festivals reinforce the religious and political order. The other type of festival is what Bakhtin calls the carnival. Bakhtin describes the carnival as the alternative or second life that medieval people enjoyed. A carnival was a completely different and a separate celebration from the official world and its festivals. Carnivals were outside of the religious and the political order. To put it in terms of the present, a graduation is an official feast, while fraternity and sorority parties demonstrate the carnival.

There are three more elements about Bakhtin's idea of the carnival that are important here. The first element is play. A carnival can be a time and a place to play with things in the official world. Bakhtin mentions that certain carnival elements play with or parody things that are taken quite seriously in the official, religious, and political worlds. Bakhtin says that the carnival world is life "shaped according to a certain pattern of play."[26]

---

26. Bakhtin, *Rabelais and His World*, 7.

Maybe

A second central element in the carnival is laughter. Bakhtin goes so far as to say that the carnival is organized on the basis of laughter. Bakhtin's carnival laughter is festive laughter. What he means by this is that it is laughter spread throughout everyone. Carnival laughter isn't one person making jokes for an audience. In the carnival, everyone is comedian and audience at the same time. Carnival laughter is everybody laughing at everybody. Everyone and everything are joyfully made fun of and mocked. He describes this laughter as ambivalent. At one moment the laughter might seem gay and triumphant but at the same time it can be mocking and deriding. Bakhtin says that carnival laughter "asserts and denies, it buries and revives."[27]

The last element of the carnival is its utopian quality. Bakhtin describes how the carnival, the second life of the people, allows them to enter "the utopian realm of community, freedom, equality, and abundance."[28] In many ways, official feasts are about scarcity. Not everyone earns a university degree. Graduation ceremonies celebrate this scarce resource and accomplishment. Official feasts reinforce a community built on inequality. Not just anyone can go sit up on the stand with the university president. Rank and status go with authority to give university degrees their meaning outside of the university. But the fraternity or sorority party is based on abundance. There is an abundance of alcohol that everyone is free to imbibe. There is a community built on the idea that everyone is equal at the party. Students enter their utopian second life when they enter this carnival. And there is one final and very important part of the carnival utopia: in order to genuinely enjoy this utopian second life, Bakhtin adds that it is a place of fearlessness.[29]

Play, laughter, and the utopian element are easy to see in the Feast of Fools in the Disney movie. Everyone is invited to leave the official world, leave their first life of daily tasks, church, and school. This world prizes ugliness and the grotesque over beauty and nobility. They also laugh abundantly, as they insult and mock religious and political authorities. In this world of community, freedom, abundance, and fearlessness, the central character, leader, and unifying force is the clown. Here everyone is a king and every king is a clown.

27. Bakhtin, *Rabelais and His World*, 11–12.
28. Bakhtin, *Rabelais and His World*, 9.
29. Bakhtin, *Rabelais and His World*, 47.

The Family at Burning Man's Carnival

Reese fully enjoys Burning Man's play, laughter, and utopian community of freedom and abundance. His father Hal—not so much. Reese relishes the carnival. Reese doesn't want to burn the man because he wants to stay in the carnival. Reese wants this second life to be his first and perhaps his only life.

Hal can't wait to leave Burning Man. Hal doesn't want the carnival's second life, or else he just does not know how to leave his first life, the official world. Right when the family arrives at Burning Man, Hal tells his youngest son, "I guess it's up to you to help me set up a protective perimeter around the camper. We'll need about forty rocks, at least the size of bowling balls."[30] When his son complains that he cannot find rocks for the protective perimeter and questions if it is even necessary, Hal responds with "Son, look, we might be in the desert, but we are still civilized people, and civilized people put up arbitrary boundaries that they will fight to the death to protect."[31] Instead of play, freedom, equality, abundance, and fearlessness, Hal feels he must dutifully protect whatever he can carve out as his.

Later in the episode, a disappointed Malcolm returns to the camper. Upset, Malcolm wonders, "Who's stupid idea was it to come here, anyway?"[32] Hal, enthusiastically agreeing, says, "I'm with you, Malcolm. We don't belong here. This place is full of freaks and weirdos. And now your mother and Jamie are out there with them doing God knows what. You're going to be okay, Malcolm, you are just like me."[33] Confused, Malcolm responds, "I am?"[34] Hal explains how they are similar: "Well, sure. They say we're stubborn, they say we're closed-minded, but I say there's nothing closed-minded about shunning ideas that make you scared and uncomfortable."[35] Hal continues, "And who cares if they say we're afraid of life? Life is scary. Life is things eating things. I say let everyone out there go ahead and eat each other. You and I we're gonna be in here, together, safe and sound."[36] Malcolm is repelled by his father's approach. Disappointed in himself,

---

30. Lauer, *Malcolm in the Middle*, 4:33–4:40.
31. Lauer, *Malcolm in the Middle*, 7:45–7:52.
32. Lauer, *Malcolm in the Middle*, 14:35.
33. Lauer, *Malcolm in the Middle*, 14:37–14:49.
34. Lauer, *Malcolm in the Middle*, 14:50.
35. Lauer, *Malcolm in the Middle*, 14:51–14:59.
36. Lauer, *Malcolm in the Middle*, 15:01–15:16.

Malcolm leaves the RV. When he leaves the camper, his upset father follows him out the door. The crowd is still there, awaiting the next scene in what they believe to be Hal's performance art parody of the suburban dad. Hal steps out of the camper and yells at Malcolm, "Where are you going? Don't walk away from me when I'm talking to you, young man!"[37] The crowd roars with approving laughter and cheers. Then, even more confused and irate, Hal flees into the safety of the camper and yells at the gathered crowd, "Get . . . off . . . my . . . property!"[38] This, of course, only elicits more cheers and laughter.

Toward the end of the episode, Hal finally gets his wish—Burning Man is coming to an end. The family will return to their normal lives. Hal pulls up to where the crowd is about to burn Burning Man. He gets out of the van, yelling for his family to get in so that they can go. Dewey, having just cleaned the mats, walks toward but does not quite reach the van. Malcolm comes back, but Hal does not let him go through the RV's open door until he cleans himself off. Lois is still celebrating, and Reese, as mentioned before, is trying to keep Burning Man going as long as possible. Reese, believing that he can delay Burning Man's end at least a little bit longer, hurls the torch he was given in the other direction. That torch happens to land right inside the open camper door, falling on volatile cleaning chemicals, and causing the entire camper to burst into flames. Everyone looks on in amazement as the fire consumes the camper. The crowd that was once chanting, "Burning Man!, Burning Man!" starts chanting, in delighted amazement, "Burning Van! Burning Van!"[39]

Hal never gets comfortable at Burning Man. Reese is perhaps too comfortable. Striking the best balance between Hal and Reese, between the official and the carnival, between her first life and her second life, is Lois. When they get to Burning Man, Lois gets out of the camper, looks around with a big smile, and announces, "Hey, neighbors! I'm gonna do art too. I brought my paintbrushes."[40] During her stay she takes Jamie to get done up by the women in her group. She is so excited about what they have done that she squeals, "Oh my gosh! This is fantastic. Oh . . . I wish there was a JC Penney nearby. I'd love to get wallets of this."[41] Later in the episode, she

37. Lauer, *Malcolm in the Middle*, 15:24–15:28.

38. Lauer, *Malcolm in the Middle*, 15:37–15:38.

39. Lauer, *Malcolm in the Middle*, 20:30–20:40.

40. Lauer, *Malcolm in the Middle*, 4:19–4:24.

41. Lauer, *Malcolm in the Middle*, 14:25–14:32.

adds food coloring to the scrambled eggs because she's being creative and artistic. By the end Lois has joined a group of topless women on bicycles known as the Trumpet Strumpets. Lois embraces the play, laughter, and utopian community, freedom, equality, fearlessness, and abundance that Burning Man offers. In the show's last scene, Reese turns to tell someone, "I still can't believe how awesome Burning Man was. Next year, we're totally going back to Burning Man."[42] Given Reese's conversation at the beginning of the episode, we assume that he's talking to Malcolm. Instead, the person who whispers an emphatic "Totally" to Reese is Lois.[43]

Malcolm does not effortlessly embrace the carnival like his mother or his brother. Nor does he lock himself in the camper like his father. One of Malcolm's first experiences at Burning Man is stepping on a cactus and injuring his foot. He ends up in a long line for traditional Western first-aid. A stranger in a buffalo mask recommends the shaman's tent, since she "totally cured his plantar warts."[44] The shaman diagnoses what she sees as his problem: "You have an incredible amount of passion in your soul. But you've got to let down the armor you're using to shield it. You also need a tetanus shot."[45] Over the course of the next few quick scenes, Malcolm and the shaman discuss alternative healing, colonizing space, the continuity of spiritual existence after death, the role of Godzilla in Japanese post-WWII guilt, the best rock-and-roll girl groups, the often-overlooked self-pity in *Charlotte's Web*, favorite foods, and their shared favorite Sesame Street character—Oscar the Grouch. They grow evermore emotionally, psychologically, and physically intimate until a post-coital Malcolm again breaks the fourth wall, looks into the camera and exclaims, "Wow, and I thought all that crap everyone said about love was just to piss me off."[46] Far from a conspiracy to piss him off, Malcolm has experienced love's emotional intimacy and physical embodiment. The shaman told him that his tremendous passion was penned in by his defensive armor. She invited him to let it down, and with his vulnerability came intimacy.

But Malcolm's bliss is short-lived. The next morning, when they start to make plans, the shaman detects that Malcolm looks down on what she does. Angry at his disrespect, she orders him to leave. It is then that Malcolm

42. Lauer, *Malcolm in the Middle*, 20:47–20:51.

43. Lauer, *Malcolm in the Middle*, 20:52.

44. Lauer, *Malcolm in the Middle*, 8:43–8:44.

45. Lauer, *Malcolm in the Middle*, 9:35–9:46.

46. Lauer, *Malcolm in the Middle*, 10:58.

flees to the camper and encounters his father. As mentioned previously, Malcolm's father's approach to Burning Man turns Malcolm off. He returns to the shaman's tent to give her rebirthing ritual a try. Here again he lets down his armor. He emerges from the experience exhilarated. He says of the experience, "I was able to open my mind and be accepting of something I didn't believe in. I've never been able to do that before. It's amazing, I actually feel like I've been reborn. It feels fantastic. And it's all thanks to you."[47] The shaman congratulates him, but then immediately proclaims, "We can never see each other again."[48] The baffled Malcolm questions why, and she explains that he's too malleable. When Malcolm still does not understand, she tells him that "Life is a journey that you have to take on your own."[49] The shaman rejects Malcolm to set him free, to push him to grow up and to become an autonomous, fully formed adult. At this moment, that is not what Malcolm wants, and he, breaking the fourth wall again, complains, "Great. Who knew this life could be even crappier than the last one?!"[50]

At Burning Man, Lois and Reese experience play, laughter, and fearlessness in a utopian community of freedom, equality, and abundance. A frightened and closed-minded Hal never experiences those things. In fact, in Hal and his boss's RV, the official world is mocked, parodied, and finally burned in effigy. Malcolm moves uneasily between embracing the carnival and rejecting it. The carnival world invites Malcolm to let down the defensive armor he uses in his first life, in the official world. This creates a new and exhilarating experience for him. When he is momentarily spurned, he returns to his father, the van, and the safety of the official. But Malcolm sees Hal's reliance on the official as narrow-minded and afraid. He again returns to embrace the carnival, and again finds the experience exhilarating and mind-altering. Still, even that experience ends in disappointment. The shaman will not take him with her. He must become a self-sufficient adult and must return to his first life.

Reese and Lois embrace the carnival. Hal does not. Malcolm goes back and forth between entering the carnival and retreating to Hal, to the official. He does not know how to embrace the carnival, but he is also repulsed by the official. Malcolm is stuck between the carnival and the official. Between Reese, who never wants the carnival to end (though it must) and Hal, who

47. Lauer, *Malcolm in the Middle*, 18:13–18:24.
48. Lauer, *Malcolm in the Middle*, 18:26.
49. Lauer, *Malcolm in the Middle*, 18:41–18:43.
50. Lauer, *Malcolm in the Middle*, 18:53–18:54.

can never leave the official and relish the carnival (though he should), Malcolm seems to find himself right where we might expect—in the middle.

So Why "Maybe?"

Malcolm is in the middle between embracing the carnival and fleeing to the official. But Lois seems to figure this out. She relishes her experience at Burning Man. She is an adult who knows how to balance her experiences in a second life with the demands of one's first life. So then why is this chapter in this book's "Maybe" section? In adolescence and perhaps early adulthood it is difficult to strike an appropriate balance. Perhaps in adulthood one can relish the carnival for what it provides. One can enjoy the carnival without wanting it to be permanent. One can make sure that the official does not keep us from the play, the laughter, the fearlessness, and the utopia of the carnival. Doesn't this seem like just the sort of healthy balance and healthy laughter that might make one's life and even the world better?

Yes, if one could always maintain such a balance and if one could always be so wise, then carnival laughter would make the world a better place. But that is not the case. It is also not the case because authorities don't like to be mocked. To explain what I mean by that, I will mention some famous or infamous fraternity and sorority parties. One was a Thanksgiving party held at California Polytechnic State University. The theme was "Colonial Bros and Nava-Hos."[51] A Harvard fraternity threw a similar party on Columbus day with the theme of "Conquistabros and Navajos."[52] If you want to look, you can find lots of offensive fraternity or sorority parties. You can find news reports and commentary from the political right, left, and center that rebuke and berate those organizations for their blatant racism, sexism, homophobia, and general offensiveness. Honestly, I only gave those two themes because the rest bothered me a lot.

And this brings us to the point about the carnival—part of the carnival is mocking religious and political authorities. In our culture, the judges of moral virtue are not limited to those ordained in religious organizations. Our authorities include those who judge the harm actions cause, often with a special eye toward those who have traditionally been harmed but have lacked power to speak up or to find redress. Carnival is a time and place, perhaps *the* time and the place, to play with cultural, social, and political

51. See Moya-Smith, "'Colonial Bros and Nava-Hos.'"
52. See K., "Harvard's 'Conquistabros and Navajos' Frat Party."

elements. That means playing with norms. It means playing with taboos in a utopian realm of laughter and fearlessness. But the reality is that the official world stands in an uneasy relationship with the carnival. Often, the best the carnival can do is remain isolated from the official. This is because if the official comes near the carnival, the official will feel compelled to police the carnival. Universities are willing to let fraternities and sororities relish the carnival until that carnival spills out too far onto campus, onto social media, or into the official world. At that point, there will be investigations, inquests, meetings, hearings, forums, white papers, campus conversations, statements, actions, sanctions, censures and so forth. If the official were close enough to what we saw in the Burning Man episode, the shaman would be arrested and prosecuted for statutory rape. There is an ideal in which the carnival and official can each have their space and can each provide something useful and valuable. While both seem inherently at odds with one another, they can complement one another. But properly enjoying what each offers, as Lois does, is an ideal that is difficult to achieve. More often, instead of taking the best of the official and the carnival, people choose one over the other. In other words, instead of striking Lois's ideal balance, people all too easily fall into either the role of Hal or the role of Reese.

CHAPTER 6

A Battle between a Humidifier and a De-humidifier

Paul Beatty's *The Sellout*

THE AMERICAN STAND-UP COMEDIAN Steven Wright tells a joke that one year for his birthday he got a humidifier and a de-humidifier. He adds that he likes to put them both in the same room and let them battle it out.[1] The American novelist Paul Beatty wrote a book that is like this fight between a humidifier and a de-humidifier. Beatty's book is called *The Sellout*, but to explain how it is like a battle between a humidifier and a de-humidifier we need to spend some time with three thinkers and their ideas about why we laugh. The three thinkers are Matthew Hurley, Daniel Dennett, and Reginald Adams.

Mirth and Error Detection

In 2004, Matthew Hurley, then an undergraduate at Tufts University, took a psychology course about theories of humor from Reginald Adams. During that semester, Hurley started to develop some ideas about why people laugh.[2] He wanted to know what evolutionary advantage laughing might give someone in a fight for survival. He developed this idea that in order to survive, you have to understand the world around you correctly. You have

1. Wright, "Ants," 44:00–57:00.
2. See McNeil, "Everyone's a Comedian."

to be able to understand if those yellow things, bananas, are a tasty treat or if they will kill you. And it isn't just bananas. You have to understand a whole lot of things: animals, cliffs, fire, childbirth, hypothermia, and non-verbal cues from your mother-in-law.

And this brings up the next problem—not only do you need to understand things correctly, but you need to constantly double-check your thinking. You might understand correctly that bananas are a tasty treat, but then you might assume that they are completely harmless. And bananas do seem harmless. But Hurley developed the idea that people evolved to get a reward every time they detect a thinking error. The reward is what he calls mirth. But what does Hurley mean by a thinking error? What does he mean by mirth? How can mirth be a reward? And how could bananas be dangerous?

To see mirth in action, imagine that you are eating delicious bananas with some mastodon-hunting friends. You believe that bananas are harmless. You and your friends are eating the bananas and then just throwing the peels around willy-nilly. Suddenly, one of your cave-dwelling colleagues puts too much weight on a slippery peel and finds themself on their back with their feet in the air. You laugh. So why did you laugh? According to Hurley, you laughed because you got a jolt of mirth. That mirth was a reward for seeing the mistake. The mistake is putting too much weight on a banana peel, but Hurley digs deeper. His idea is that you were rewarded with mirth not just for detecting the obvious mistake, but as a reward for detecting a deeper mistake. That mistake was the idea that bananas are completely harmless. This little situation revealed to you that not only can bananas be dangerous, but your thinking was wrong. In fact, the mirth you felt reinforced the lesson. Now, in the future, you will be careful around banana peels. You will also be a little bit more careful about all of your assumptions. Being careful helps you avoid little things like slipping on a banana peel, but it can also help you avoid much more serious mistakes.

Matthew Hurley worked with his course's instructor, Reginald Adams, and with Daniel Dennett to develop his idea that laughter comes from the mirth we experience when we detect a thinking error. He presented an early version of this idea in his honors thesis. His mentors were so impressed that the three of them worked together and eventually published *Inside Jokes: Using Humor to Reverse-Engineer the Mind*. In this book, these authors look inside different jokes to see what is happening. They examine jokes to see how they inspire the jolt of mirth you get when you detect an error.[3]

3. Hurley et al., *Inside Jokes*, 127.

To be clear, here are two examples of how laughter comes from the mirth you get as a reward for error detection. Around 200 BCE, the Roman playwright Plautus wrote a comedy called "The Swaggering Soldier" or "The Braggart Soldier." The play features a slave who wins his freedom by taking advantage of the arrogance of the swaggering, bragging soldier. One thing that is funny about the play is seeing the arrogant soldier tricked, beaten, and embarrassed. Perhaps this idea for a comedy, a play about one man's arrogance being popped like a bubble, seems familiar. We laugh at the errors of arrogant men like Ralph Kramden in *The Honeymooners*, Archie Bunker in *All in the Family*, and Michael Scott in *The Office*, just to name a few. What Hurley, Adams, and Dennett might say about these comedies is that they show the thinking errors of men who don't really understand themselves. These men put on shows of greatness but lack the qualities to back up those shows. The play and the sitcoms are carefully crafted to reveal in interesting and surprising ways the main characters' thinking errors. We, the audience, see those errors, we are rewarded with mirth for having detected them, and we laugh.

Short Note about Sex

It might be clear that to survive you need to understand the world correctly. And it might be clear that we sometimes laugh when we see someone make a mistake, like slipping on a banana peel. And okay, it is funny to watch people make mistakes, like Michael Scott or countless online videos that start with a man saying: "Hold my beer." But if mirth is supposed to help us think better and not make mistakes, why do we have comedies? Why do we have plays, television shows, movies, books, and so many other things that make us laugh? Have we made all of that stuff so we can detect errors and think better? Are we trying to reveal every possible thinking error? Are we deliberately creating humorous material in our quest to form the smartest human beings that could possibly evolve?

Hurley et al. have an interesting answer for that question. They compare laughter and error detection with sex.[4] In order for humans to survive, we have to reproduce. But, if you think about it, having children is difficult, risky, and expensive. These three thinkers note that humans evolved to have a reward associated with reproduction. Sex is fun. In fact, sex is so fun

---

4. Hurley et al., *Inside Jokes*, 127–28.

that people forget the dangers and costs of having children. Or at least they forget momentarily.

But nowadays, sex isn't just a reward to get you to reproduce. Today we use the rewards associated with sex for their own sake. In fact, we use sex to advertise almost anything you can sell, from hamburgers to cars. There is even an accidently hilarious commercial that uses the very sexy Eva Longoria to sell . . . wait for it . . . cat food. The rewards associated with sex have been manipulated to get you to do something else. We have plays, television shows, movies, books, and so many other things that turn us on to the rewards associated with reproduction for the pleasure of the reward itself and not to get us to reproduce.

Hurley et al. say that just as the rewards associated with having children have been used for other things, so the rewards associated with error detection have been used for their own sake. Comedians and others make sure you detect the error in just the right way, with a mixture of the familiar and a surprise, so that you get the rewarding mirth. I doubt it is making us that much smarter for all of our error detection. We just like the mirth that comes as a reward for doing it.

A Place for Error Detection and Mirth

Hurley et al. do something very interesting and dangerous in their book. As they attempt to get inside of jokes, they explain how jokes strike us as funny. And strike is the right word, because it is as if a joke's punchline hits you. They examine what hits you, why it hits you, and why some jokes are not that funny.

One of their ideas is that in your daily life, you create what they call mental spaces.[5] A mental space is a place where you are thinking about what is happening right in front of you. You bring together what you perceive as well as your working memory to make sense of the world and to make predictions. Mental spaces are created bit by bit, you are constantly adjusting and tweaking them, and they are used to predict what will happen next. Jokes play in mental spaces, and they play with your attempts to make useful and accurate predictions. To show this in action, Hurley et al. mention examples like when you have waited for an instant replay only to suddenly recall that you are at a live game.[6] You try to bring a pattern that

5. Hurley et al., *Inside Jokes*, 117–22.
6. Hurley et al., *Inside Jokes*, 132.

you use somewhere, like seeing a replay on television at home, and you mistakenly try to use that approach somewhere else—at a live game. You see the mistake you've made and chuckle to yourself.

Here is another joke that the authors examine: "Do you mind telling me why you ran away from the operating room?" the hospital administrator asked the patient. "Because the nurse said, 'Don't be afraid! An appendectomy is quite simple.'" "So?" questioned the administrator. "So?" exclaimed the patient, "She was talking to the surgeon!"[7] Okay, that is not a great joke, but if you take a moment to think about this joke, if you slow down and try to get inside it, you can see that the set-up creates a mental space. The set-up prompts you to picture a patient speaking with a hospital administrator sometime after the patient had fled from a common surgery. The set-up also relies on the notion that you will commit yourself to believing not just that the surgery is routine and simple, but that the nurse was reassuring a nervous patient. In this mental space, you might predict that some unfounded fears on the part of the patient caused that person to act irrationally. That is a logical way you create this mental space and make predictions about it. But then the punchline reveals that your prediction was based on faulty assumptions. You assumed that the nurse was reassuring the patient, when in reality she was reassuring the surgeon. The nurse's need to reassure the surgeon makes the fears and subsequent flight of the patient suddenly real and rational. The jolt of mirth that accompanied the punchline was your reward for detecting the errors you made in creating the mental space and in making predictions based on your assumptions.

Whitey Week and the "Bystander Effect"

Mental spaces, error detection, and mirth are all over Paul Beatty's book *The Sellout*, and many of them center around racism in the United States. One way the book talks about race is to talk about white people and whiteness. The narrator does not give his first name, but since one nickname for him is Bonbon, we'll use that. Toward the end of the book, Bonbon and the middle school's assistant principal, Charisma Molina, create what they call "Whitey Week." Bonbon describes it as a "moment of respite for children forced to participate in classroom reenactments of stories of migrant labor, illegal immigration, and the Middle Passage."[8] He goes on to explain that it

7. Hurley et al., *Inside Jokes*, 168.
8. Beatty, *Sellout*, 226.

was for kids who are "weary and stuffed from being force-fed the false-hood that when one of your kind makes it, it means that you've all made it."[9] What Bonbon and Charisma do is convert a closed-down, brushless carwash into what they call a "tunnel of whiteness."[10] They then alter the carwash signs to give the children "several race options:"

> Regular Whiteness: Benefit of the Doubt
> > Higher Life Expectancy
> > Lower Insurance Premiums
> Deluxe Whiteness: Regular Whiteness Plus
> > Warnings Instead of Arrests from the Police
> > Decent Seats at Concerts and Sporting Events
> > World Revolves Around You and Your Concerns
> Super Deluxe Whiteness: Deluxe Whiteness Plus
> > Jobs with Annual Bonuses
> > Military Service Is for Suckers
> > Legacy Admission to College of Your Choice
> > Therapists That Listen
> > Boats That You Never Use
> > All Vices and Bad Habits Referred to as "Phases"
> > Not Responsible for Scratches, Dents, and Items Left in the Subconscious[11]

Bonbon and Charisma finish their activity by allowing the kids to dance and laugh in the carwash's hot water and suds followed by letting them stand in the hot-air blowers. Describing this last part of the activity, Bonbon says that "reminding (the kids) that having a warm wind blow-ing in your face was what it felt like to be white and rich. That life for the fortunate few was like being in the front seat of a convertible twenty-four hours a day."[12]

We can examine this episode with Hurley et al.'s ideas about laughter. We know about events like Black History or Hispanic Heritage months. We can put them in a mental space with certain expectations. But "Whitey Week" does not match those expectations. "Whitey Week" is about white people, and it is a week and not a month. In addition, unlike the patterns established by Black History and Hispanic Heritage months, Whitey Week isn't serious or important. It is fun and seemingly frivolous. In fact, it is

9. Beatty, *Sellout*, 226–27.
10. Beatty, *Sellout*, 227.
11. Beatty, *Sellout*, 227.
12. Beatty, *Sellout*, 228.

described as a break from the seriousness of the celebrations. The author creates an interesting mental space that combines a carwash with privileges enjoyed by white people. The list of race options, when compared to carwash options, reinforces how racial privilege and wealth gets you more stuff. With each addition comes all of the benefits of the previous, so as you move up in wealth you get more added to what you already have. This activity shows the schoolchildren and readers what might not be obvious in everyday life—how race and class give some people inherent advantages. In the mental space shared by Black History and Hispanic Heritage months, a carwash, and privileges enjoyed by wealthy white people, the otherwise invisible reality and folly of rich, white privilege, is clear. Hopefully you detected those thwarted expectations, thinking errors, and follies as you read. And hopefully you laughed.

The Sellout isn't just about privileges enjoyed by wealthy white people. Most of it is about racism's impact on its survivors and not its beneficiaries. In addition, a lot of what Bonbon examines has to do with his father. Bonbon's father, a psychologist, homeschooled him in such a way that he might be perfectly suited to respond to racism. Ever the scientist, part of that preparation included his father replicating famous experiments. Bonbon tells us, for instance, that when he was eight his father used him to test the "bystander effect."[13] The bystander effect is the idea that when more people are around to help, bystanders actually help less, assuming others will step in. But Bonbon's father believed that this didn't apply to black people, who are "a loving race whose very survival has been dependent on helping one another in times of need."[14]

To test this hypothesis, Bonbon's father had him "stand on the busiest intersection in the neighborhood, dollar bills bursting from my pockets, the latest and shiniest electronic gadgetry jammed into my ear canals, a hip-hop heavy gold chain hanging from my neck, and, inexplicably, a set of custom-made carpeted Honda Civic floor mats draped over my forearm like a waiter's towel."[15] Bonbon's father then proceeded to mug him. Bonbon says, "He beat me down in front of a throng of bystanders, who didn't stand by for long."[16] Bonbon creates a mental space, and we bring our expectations to that space. But he continues, "The mugging wasn't two

13. Beatty, *Sellout*, 29.
14. Beatty, *Sellout*, 30.
15. Beatty, *Sellout*, 30.
16. Beatty, *Sellout*, 30.

punches to the face old when the people came, not to my aid, but to my father's. Assisting him in my ass kicking, they happily joined in with flying elbows and television wrestling throws."[17] After the beating was over, Bonbon tells us that "On the way home, Pops put a consoling arm around my aching shoulders and delivered an apologetic lecture about his failure to take into account the 'bandwagon effect.'"[18]

This second episode from the book invites us to enter a mental space and to believe with Bonbon's father that blacks inherently help other blacks. To add to the drama of this mental space, we see how Bonbon's father has stereotypically and outrageously outfitted him to be mugged. We are invited to go along with the outcome predicted by the experiment's designer and principle actor—Bonbon's father. But in this mental space, those predictions prove mistaken. And, to heighten the erroneous predictions, Bonbon's father does not console him like we might expect a loving father to do. Instead, he ignores the human impact of the experiment. He views what has happened strictly as a scientist, noting the presence of a mitigating scientific principle—the bandwagon effect.

Bonbon suffers through many similarly failed experiments that his father designed. Bonbon, however, has little interest in science but does seem to have a remarkable skill for farming. Because people expect him to be like his father, and because of his childhood love of *The Little Rascals*, and because of his genuine kindness toward the vulnerable, Bonbon ends up owning a slave. You know. You will see what I mean when you read the book, but just from that sentence, you can see that the book plays with lots and lots of mental spaces, predictions, expectations, and thinking errors. And the book is very funny.

Bonbon's father and the people close to him seem to expect Bonbon to carry on their work. That work is ending racism. But Bonbon, as explored in the book, does not seem to buy into key principles in that work. Because he does not buy in, he is called "the sellout." At the very end of the book, a black comedian chases a white couple from a predominantly black comedy and night club. The comedian yells for the couple to leave saying, "Get out. This is our thing."[19] Looking back on the incident, Bonbon wished he would have stood up and said something. He doesn't wish he would have stood up for the couple, "but I wish I'd stood up to the man and asked him a

17. Beatty, *Sellout*, 30.
18. Beatty, *Sellout*, 30.
19. Beatty, *Sellout*, 287.

question: 'So what exactly is our thing?'"[20] Bonbon cannot put his finger on exactly what the Black thing is. Put another way, he cannot find the essence of blackness. He either wants the comedian to explain it, or he wants to show how it is a thinking error.

The Sellout calls out racism. It calls it out in many, many instances. The example we've noted—one of many—is white privilege as seen in Whitey Week. As the book fights racism, it is doing an important work. It is like a humidifier. *The Sellout* also calls out idealized versions of black people. The book examines efforts like his father's failed attempt to prove that Blacks inherently help one another. As the book questions idealized or assimilationist versions of black people, and as it questions an essential black thing, it is also doing an important work. That work is like a de-humidifier. A book that questions what blackness is while also fighting racism can be confusing. Beatty's book humorously points out many conflicting thinking errors. And, since those errors are in the novel's same mental space, the entire novel can feel like the room Steven Wright described: a room where a humidifier and de-humidifier battle it out.

20. Beatty, *Sellout*, 288.

CHAPTER 7

The Lists Chapter

An Arrest Gone Wrong

THE ARREST DIDN'T GO well. The police officer had finally found what looked like a truly suspicious character—an oafish guy in a plaid flannel shirt, tweed trousers, a muffler, and a green hunting cap in always-warm-and-muggy New Orleans. He looked fishy even in the Big Easy. The police officer asked him for his driver's license, but the man, Ignatius, said he didn't drive. The officer noticed something hanging out of his bag. When he asked him what it was, Ignatius's sarcastic reply was, "What do you think it is, stupid? It's a string to my lute."[1] Patrolman Mancuso regained his composure and pushed forward with more questions. The annoyed Ignatius bellowed out, "Is it part of the police department to harass me when the city is a flagrant vice capital of the civilized world?"[2] What Ignatius said next gets us into the focus of this chapter:

> This city is famous for its gamblers, prostitutes, exhibitionists, Antichrists, alcoholics, sodomites, drug addicts, fetishists, onanists, pornographers, frauds, jades, litter bugs, and lesbians, all of whom are only too well protected by graft. If you have a moment, I shall endeavor to discuss the crime problem with you, but don't make the mistake of bothering *me*.[3]

---

1. Toole, *Confederacy of Dunces*, 3.
2. Toole, *Confederacy of Dunces*, 3.
3. Toole, *Confederacy of Dunces*, 3 (italics original).

Ignatius J. Reilly has quite a catalog of the vices in New Orleans, and he rattles that list off for Patrolman Mancuso in the first three pages of John Kennedy Toole's novel *A Confederacy of Dunces*. It turns out that the list foreshadows many of the characters we'll meet in the novel. And while Ignatius seems to be above all of this depravity and vice, that word squirreled away in the middle, "onanist," happens to describe Ignatius. If you are not familiar, Onan was the Old Testament man who failed to fulfill his cultural obligation of getting his deceased brother's wife pregnant. At the crucial moment, Onan spilled his seed. From that fraternal failure and with a lot of interpretive stretching, over time the sin of Onan came to mean masturbation. Ignatius is happy to consult with the police about his city's vice problem, but perhaps they should not ask too many questions.

We learn from Ignatius's list that he looks down on the people in his hometown. He scorns their weakness and vice but buries his own shortcomings. We learn more about Ignatius when the officer asks him if he has a job. His mother intervenes that Ignatius has to help around the house because of her arthritis. Ignatius claims that, "I dust a bit," but his real defense is this: "I am at the moment writing a lengthy indictment against our century. When my brain begins to reel from my literary labors, I make an occasional cheese dip."[4]

The gap between Ignatius's lengthy indictment against our century and his cheese dip and the gap between how Ignatius looks down on others while denying his own flaws—those are the gaps that make Ignatius interesting. Those gaps help make this book funny. And it is in Ignatius's lists that we find these gaps. To expand on how lists make the book funny and reveal its interesting gaps, here are some additional lists.

Ignatius writes his indictments against his century in pencil on Big Chief writing tablets. He longs for an idealized medieval past. He writes, "After a period in which the western world had enjoyed order, tranquility, unity, and oneness with its True God and Trinity, there appeared winds of change which spelled evil days ahead."[5] Ignatius elaborates on the loss of order, tranquility, unity, and oneness when he says, "The luminous years of Abelard, Thomas à Beckett, and Everyman dimmed into dross; Fortuna's wheel had turned on humanity, crushing its collarbone, smashing its skull, twisting its torso, puncturing its pelvis, sorrowing its soul."[6] Igna-

---

4. Toole, *Confederacy of Dunces*, 6.
5. Toole, *Confederacy of Dunces*, 28.
6. Toole, *Confederacy of Dunces*, 28.

tius lists the heroes of the medieval past—Abelard, Thomas à Beckett, and Everyman. When he describes how Fortune has turned on humanity, he offers crushed collarbones, punctured pelvises, and sorrowed souls in his exaggerated, flowery, and accidentally hilarious list. Ignatius finishes with two more quips that use alliteration and word play: "Having once been so high, humanity fell so low. What had once been dedicated to the soul was now dedicated to the sale."[7] When Ignatius admires what he has written, he concludes, "That is rather fine."[8]

It is also rather funny. Ignatius sees himself as a highly intellectual, moral medievalist forced to witness humanity's depravity in a century where he does not belong. His lists express this, and they make him sound systematic and thorough. He is a lofty and clear mind of truth. Yes, his indictment is overly dramatic. And yes, it is transcribed in pencil on Big Chief tablets. And Ignatius's mind is in a body that craves Dr. Nut soda, consumes dozens of hot dogs, and needs a more than occasional cheese dip. And yes, that body and soul will sometimes seek solace in the sensual siren song that is the sin of Onan. And as we compare what Ignatius thinks of himself and what he's really like, it is the contrast that makes this humorous. And it is the lists that make those contrasts vivid.

A Fella Could Have a Pretty Good Time in Vegas with All That Stuff

This next list is supposed to save your life. It is a list of items in a small metal box. You and your fellow pilots have identical boxes. Before you face what could be the end of your life, you double-check the list and the items in your survival kit. You are about to start a life-or-death mission. The fate of your country is a stake. You can even hear the quiet drumming and a harmonica playing "When Johnny Comes Marching Home" in the background. The bomber's commanding officer, Major Kong, reads the instructions, and the other airmen check their survival kits. Major Kong reads the list with a thick Texas drawl. The first items make sense—a firearm, ammunition, and "four days concentrated emergency rations."[9] So far so good—a weapon to defend yourself and food to stay alive. Check. Next come medicines, including antibiotics, morphine, and vitamins. Solid emergency medical

7. Toole, *Confederacy of Dunces*, 28.
8. Toole, *Confederacy of Dunces*, 28.
9. Kubrick, *Dr. Strangelove*, 35:49–35:52.

supplies—good idea. But the survival kit also has "pep pills, sleepin' pills, tranquilizer pills."[10] That is a lot of pills! Of course pills are light and don't take up much space, so I guess they make sense. The next item is where things get odd. The survival kit contains a "miniature combination Russian phrase book and Bible."[11] An airman inspects this book, the camera points right at him, and the book looks to be about one inch square. That is a very small phrase book and Bible. Next the airmen double-check their survival kits for one hundred dollars in Russian rubles and one hundred dollars in gold. It looks like the "survival" that this kit imagines would be in Russia or at least with people taking Russian money. It does have gold as a sort of universal backup.

It is the next item that tells us that something is not right—nine packs of chewing gum. That is a lot of gum! In a kit that can only fit a very small phrase book and Bible, gum certainly seems like a surprising and a space-consuming addition. The next item is an "issue of prophylactics."[12] A prophylactic is something that prevents disease, but here an "issue of prophylactics" is a government phrase and bureaucratic euphemism for a pack of condoms. After the condoms come the survival kit's last and most unexpected items—"three lipsticks, three pair of nylon stockings."[13] Even Major Kong notices a trend at this point, commenting that "Shoot, a fella could have a pretty good weekend in Vegas with all that stuff."[14]

While it would be great for Vegas, you are not lasting very long in the woods with the survival kit in Stanley Kubrick's 1964 black comedy *Dr. Strangelove or: How I Learned to Stop Worrying and Love the Bomb*. Forget the woods—it sounds like this is a survival kit for pilots parachuting into a brothel. From the movie we know the man or at least the sort of men who made this survival kit. The movie's generals have affairs and, when nervous or sexually frustrated, chew gum. They start wars because they believe that their enemies are trying to make them sexually powerless. They comfort themselves that even if there is atomic annihilation, they will survive in converted mine shafts where they will enjoy a ten-to-one female-to-male ratio as they repopulate the world.

10. Kubrick, *Dr. Strangelove*, 35:59–36:03.
11. Kubrick, *Dr. Strangelove*, 36:04–36:08.
12. Kubrick, *Dr. Strangelove*, 36:17–36:18.
13. Kubrick, *Dr. Strangelove*, 36:20–36:23.
14. Kubrick, *Dr. Strangelove*, 36:24–36:28.

Maybe

If those sexual elements were not clear enough, the movie includes a lot of phallic symbols, starting with the very first shot of the refueling plane. Cigars and large guns are obviously sexual, and having sex is compared to a rocket blastoff. The event that finally starts atomic destruction is a hooting and howling cowboy riding an outrageous and humorously sexual atomic bomb.

The survival kit brings together all of the things Kubrick's movie is humorously attacking. The kit starts out seemingly normal—weapon, food, medicine. The Cold War might also seem normal. That war might just be a modern version of military conflicts that humans have had since the beginning. But Kubrick points out that this conflict, perhaps like those of the past, is about men showing sexual domination over other men and over women. Because of nuclear weapons and the devastation they can cause, the Cold War forces men to stop fighting and cool down. But men like Jack D. Ripper and Buck Turgidson hate this cool passivity. They want to warm things up. They want to end the military and sexual frustration, and they want to do it . . . with a bang. The survival kit includes the essentials men will need to survive and to beat out other men competing for sex. And there are some lipsticks and nylons thrown in as well.

Kubrick's list shows what the movie satirizes—political and military conflict as thinly disguised male sexual competition. The list starts with elements of military conflict but then twists into the competitive and sexual essentials. It moves from the commonplace to the bizarre as a way to reveal the bizarre that is otherwise hidden behind the commonplace.

The survival kit and Ignatius's lists show us one more thing—lists convey values. The men value survival, but survival based on competition with other men for sexual control of women. Ignatius's lists show how he sees himself as an outsider with a medieval moral standard taking the measure of the modern world's moral failure. Both lists tell us something that the list makers do not see themselves. The generals value their own self-preservation, control, and pleasure over people or the nation they are supposed to protect. Ignatius does not see that he is just as much a participant as the people he labels and looks down upon. The cleverness of the lists is how they say two different things at once—the messages that Ignatius and the generals intend and the messages they unknowingly convey.

Laughter and the Familiar Landmarks of Thought

Maybe you learned this list this way: "Dear King Philip Came Over For Good Soup." Or maybe you learned this one: "Do Kindly Place Cover On Fresh Green Spring Vegetables." Or maybe your biology class came up with their own mnemonic to remember "Domain, Kingdom, Phylum, Class, Order, Family, Genus, Species," and sometimes "Variety." However you remembered it, the idea was for you to understand the world of plants and animals. And the man we have to thank (or curse) for that list, that system, is Carl Linnaeus.

Carl Linnaeus was a Swede living in the 1700s. That time saw an explosion of new plant and animal species, especially from the New World. Linnaeus was unsatisfied with the then current system of animal and plant classification, so he invented his own. The old and unreliable system often gave animals and plants impossibly long names. Linnaeus set up a new system organized around physical similarities. Linnaeus's categories move from the largest and most general to the most specific and narrow. They end up looking like a tree, with lots and lots of organisms in the "Domain" region narrowing down to the fewest in the "Species" category. The largest branches in "Domain" reduce down to the smallest "Species" twigs.

Linnaeus's system was revolutionary in its time. It organized living things into a system that was orderly and useful. As new plants or animals were discovered, they could be placed within Linnaeus's system. Over time, the system has been modified and tweaked, but it is still how biologists organize the natural world. Linnaeus's system is known as a taxonomy. It is an elaborate set of embedded lists, and those lists help us understand and organized the natural world.

In 1952, the Argentinian writer Jorge Luis Borges wrote an essay about John Wilkins. Wilkins wanted to develop a universal language, something that was orderly as well as easy to learn and understand. In the essay, Borges notes that systems like the one Wilkins wanted would not be as clear, concrete, and orderly as they dreamed. Wilkins wanted a system or a taxonomy for language that was like the one Linnaeus created for plants and animals. But Borges argues that Wilkins's system, and for that matter any taxonomy, would inevitably have parts that were missing, redundant, or vague and ambiguous. For Borges, Linnaeus's and Wilkins's dreams of completeness were an illusion.

To make his point about systems and taxonomies being vague, redundant, and missing important parts, Borges provides a classification system.

He claims that this animal classification system came from a Chinese ency-clopedia and had been translated by Franz Kuhn. It is called the "Celestial Emporium of Benevolent Knowledge." Here are the categories for the ani-mals in that system:

> (a) belonging to the Emperor, (b) embalmed, (c) tame, (d) sucking pigs, (e) sirens, (f) fabulous, (g) stray dogs, (h) included in the present classification, (i) frenzied, (j) innumerable, (k) drawn with a very fine camelhair brush, (l) et cetera, (m) having just broken the water pitcher, (n) that from a long way off look like flies.[15]

Borges probably invented this classification system, and he certainly meant for it to be funny. Where Linnaeus's system looks like a tree branch-ing out and becoming more specific in an orderly fashion, this emporium is humorously random and vague. Some animals are arranged by ownership, like "belonging to the Emperor" or "stray dogs." Some categories describe the states of animals, like "embalmed," "tame," or "frenzied." Some animals are specific and cute, like "sucking pigs," but right next to them are the mermaids that sang in order to draw sailors to their deaths—"sirens." One category is "innumerable," but another one is the very specific "drawn with a very fine camelhair brush." Some animals included in the list "from a long way off look like flies," while others have "just broken a water pitcher."

One thing that makes systems like Linnaeus's taxonomy so satisfy-ing is how they bring order and organization. Linnaeus's system offers a sense of completeness and of putting everything in its right place. Borges's alternative system makes fun of that. Borges includes categories like "in-cluded in the present classification" and an "et cetera" category in his mock system. It is uselessly redundant to have a category for everything that is already included in the taxonomy. It is equally absurd to have an "et ce-tera" category, which literally means "and other things" or "and so forth." This vague, catch-all category goes against the order and completeness that systems are supposed to offer. What makes that item even funnier is that it doesn't come at the end. It might make sense as an "and anything else I might not know or have forgotten" category, but after "et cetera" come two very specific and absurd categories.

Borges's alternative system makes fun of all systems, taxonomies, and human attempts to order and organize reality. It is exaggerated and funny, yes, but it can also invite us to look critically at the systems we use

15. Borges, *Other Inquisitions*, 103.

to understand and interpret the world. It can invite us to question what we might believe is the natural order of things.

In fact, for at least one writer, that is exactly what Borges's humorous taxonomy did. And that writer was the French philosopher Michel Foucault. Foucault's book, *The Order of Things,* starts with this sentence: "This book first arose out of a passage in Borges, out of the laughter that shattered, as I read the passage, all the familiar landmarks of thought."[16] When Foucault read Borges's alternative taxonomy, his parody of the lists we use to make sense of the world, Foucault said that it broke "up all the ordered surfaces and all of the planes with which we are accustomed to tame the wild profusion of existing things."[17] That list destroyed the common ground we use to put things together in an orderly, meaningful way. Foucault takes advantage of this breaking up. His book questions what seems obvious or natural because of the systems we use. Foucault uses this laughter-inspired breaking up to reexamine the history of scientific, economic, and linguistic knowledge.

Borges's alternative taxonomy, his list, humorously invites us to question all lists. It invites us to question all of the categories we use to make sense of the world. It would be interesting to imagine what Ignatius might do with Borges's list. He might just dismiss it as absurd. He might conclude that Borges demonstrates the decay of the modern world in contrast with the order, tranquility, and unity of the past. Ignatius certainly seems certain, and certainly seems insulated against questioning his own thinking. I imagine that the generals assembling the survival kits would also be unimpressed with that bizarre list. I doubt that they would see the connection between Borges's absurd list and their own odd survival kits. Ignatius and the generals probably would not see Borges's humorous list as a criticism of their own lists and ways of creating order. Borges's list would not inspire the laughter that would cause them to question their values and how they make sense of the world.

The "Celestial Emporium of Benevolent Knowledge" probably would not shatter Ignatius or the generals' familiar landmarks of thought, but maybe humorous lists do that for audiences and readers. Perhaps the laughter brought on by these lists helps us question how we see the world. We question how Ignatius sees and fails to see the world around him. We see how Ignatius sees and fails to correctly see himself. The listed items in the survival kit show us how the generals understand and misunderstand

16. Foucault, *Order of Things*, xv.
17. Foucault, *Order of Things*, xv.

themselves and the world around them. Perhaps the lists and the laughter they inspire invite us to question what we see and how we see, especially how we understand ourselves. Maybe these humorous lists invite us to see the world better. Or maybe not.

CHAPTER 8

Edged Tools and the Death of a Branch Manager

Death of a . . .

HE'S TELLING HIS FATHER goodbye, or at least trying to. His dour and distracted father wanders around the kitchen, avoiding his defeated thirtysomething son's gaze and final handshake. His mother tries to persuade his father to acknowledge him, but the father refuses. The son turns to leave, but before he can, his father brings up the job again. He reminds his son that he had an appointment. The son tells him that there was no appointment or job, and that it was all a sham. Just as the son starts to leave, the father says, "Spite see?"[1] Spite. The father, Willy, yells the accusation that his son is leaving out of spite toward his father. Now furious, Willy screams that he is not taking the blame for his son's spiteful self-destruction. He goes so far as to blame his son for trying to put a knife in him.

You might find yourself a little lost right here. Why is the father, Willy, so hung up on his son's job and appointment? Why is Willy accusing his son, Biff, of leaving for spite and trying to put a knife in him?

This is the climactic moment in Arthur Miller's play *Death of a Salesman*. Willy's response to Biff is confusing. What Willy wants is a fight with Biff. Accusing Biff of trying to kill Willy does the trick. Earlier in the play, Biff found evidence that Willy was contemplating suicide. Willy is trying to kill himself, but here Willy is accusing Biff of killing him. Biff snaps. He pulls from his pocket a section of rubber pipe and slams it on the table. This pipe is irrefutable evidence that Willy was contemplating if not planning

---

1. Miller, *Death of a Salesman*, 129.

suicide by asphyxiation. And what does Willy do when Biff puts it on the kitchen table? He says, "What is that? I never saw that."[2] Willy looks away from the rubber pipe. Willy turns a blind eye to that object, the same blind eye he had when Biff initially tried to leave. This moment tells us a lot about Willy—Willy only sees what he wants to see.

Once Willy provokes Biff, Biff tries to break through Willy's willful blindness. The pipe is Biff's first attempt to do so. It is concrete, physical evidence, but Willy still denies it. Biff's next effort is when he accuses the entire family of constant dishonesty. Biff says that "We never told the truth for ten minutes in this house!"[3] His brother Happy refutes this by saying, "We always told the truth!"[4] Biff shoots him down, saying, "You big blow, are you the assistant buyer? You're one of the two assistants to the assistant, aren't you?"[5] Happy's anemic response is, "Well, I'm practically . . ." before Biff cuts him off and says "You're practically full of it! We all are!"[6]

Biff then tells the truth about where he has been and what has happened to him in the intervening years. Biff's inflated self-image prevented him from embracing the things he enjoyed and from accepting help from others. What Biff can see now is that his inflated self-image held him back from growth, from freedom, and from genuine satisfaction.

Biff wants to cut through Willy's and the family's self-delusions and willful blindness. The metaphorical pin he uses to burst these delusions is this phrase: "Pop! I'm a dime a dozen, and so are you!"[7] This phrase sends Willy into an uncontrolled outburst. He shrieks back at his son "I am not a dime a dozen! I am Willy Loman, and you are Biff Loman!"[8]

At this moment Biff and Willy take different paths. Biff embraces the painful realizations about who he is. He no longer sees himself as a "leader of men,"[9] as someone who will be bringing home any more prizes. Biff aspires to be another "hard-working drummer,"[10] though perhaps somebody who will not land in the trashcan like so many others. He hopes that

2. Miller, *Death of a Salesman*, 130.

3. Miller, *Death of a Salesman*, 131.

4. Miller, *Death of a Salesman*, 131.

5. Miller, *Death of a Salesman*, 131.

6. Miller, *Death of a Salesman*, 131.

7. Miller, *Death of a Salesman*, 132.

8. Miller, *Death of a Salesman*, 132.

9. Miller, *Death of a Salesman*, 133.

10. Miller, *Death of a Salesman*, 133.

living truthfully will bring him the growth, freedom, and satisfaction he has missed. But this is not an optimistic moment. Biff's despair and fury burn themselves out, and he is reduced to tears. Collapsed and weeping, he says "Pop, I'm nothing!"[11] Biff wants all of the false, phony old dreams and delusions burned and destroyed "before something happens."[12]

Willy takes an opposite path. Willy is initially enraged at Biff. He calls him a "vengeful, spiteful mutt."[13] Willy takes everything that Biff says as an accusation and an attempt to belittle and destroy him. Willy defends himself against this attack. Then, as the once-passionate, enraged Biff is burnt out and reduced to tears, Willy asks "What're you doing?"[14] An exhausted and broken Biff goes upstairs, leaving Willy and the rest of the family in the kitchen. What does Willy do? What does he conclude? As his son disappears upstairs, Willy says: "Isn't it—isn't it remarkable? Biff—he likes me!"[15] After all that has happened, Willy assembles the evidence in front of him and draws this self-deluded and willfully blind conclusion.

I start with this climactic moment from *Death of a Salesman* because it is an elegant and dramatic cautionary tale about dishonesty, self-delusion, and willful blindness. Sadly, by the end of the play, something happens that is as terrible as Biff had feared. But the play's tragedy is not limited to Willy's suicide. The play brilliantly illustrates the consequences of Willy's self-delusion and willful blindness in his life and in the lives of the people closest to him. Willy never sees his son for who he is. Willy only sees Biff as a projection of his own dreams and aspirations. When Biff tries to make Willy actually see him, Willy accuses Biff of spite. When Biff tearfully breaks down, Willy cannot see how broken Biff is. Willy cannot appreciate the courage and risk Biff has taken in trying to speak and live truthfully. Willy twists what he sees into something to make himself into what he wants to be. Willy wants to be well-liked. He is willing to sacrifice the truth about himself and about his son in order to maintain his illusion.

---

11. Miller, *Death of a Salesman*, 133.

12. Miller, *Death of a Salesman*, 133.

13. Miller, *Death of a Salesman*, 132.

14. Miller, *Death of a Salesman*, 133.

15. Miller, *Death of a Salesman*, 133.

. . . Branch Manager

To better understand Willy and self-deception, we need to talk about some-one else. And we need to talk about two thank-yous.

This is the second office meeting of the day, but whereas the first one may have been an annoying interruption, this one is a crisis. Financial ca-lamity might close this regional office of America's great paper company, Dunder Mifflin. A frantic Michael Scott wants his employees to think of a plan that will be a golden ticket idea to get them out of a mess. This second office meeting has come about because of the first. At the earlier meeting, Michael Scott, dressed as Willy Wonka, announced his golden ticket pro-motion where customers who received special golden tickets would get a discount on their next order. Michael was very excited about his brilliant idea, until their largest customer got all five tickets and would be getting a 50 percent discount on a very large order. The revenue loss threatens to close the branch.

It is in this second meeting, the one where Michael wants an idea to get him out of the mess that he's made, that Michael says the first of the episode's two thank-yous. He does not accept blame for what has happened, claiming that the promotion idea came because he is "just a net that traps all of your crappy subconscious ideas and adds a little bit of my own childhood memories and whimsy."[16] Jim announces that he's going to call corporate headquarters to explain why he lost so much of his sales. Michael seems to take Jim's plan as a golden ticket idea, a way of explaining the situation to headquarters and thereby remedying it. Seizing on Jim's response, Michael proclaims, "Thank you—Jim is with me."[17] Jim has to clarify that he is not with Michael. He is mad at Michael for causing him to lose so much money. Michael then turns this around, claiming that Jim's greed results from his overspending on a house to impress Pam. Michael is angry at Jim for not supporting his efforts to find a solution that does not involve Michael tak-ing the blame for what he has done.

This first thank-you is not as strong or important as the second. Af-ter Dwight takes what seems like the fall for Michael's initial golden ticket idea, it turns out that the idea has won the company a very lucrative con-tract. Dwight is praised by the entire office and by corporate representative David Wallace. To make matters worse, Dwight uses Michael's signature

16. Einhorn, *Office*, 7:33–7:45.
17. Einhorn, *Office*, 7:50–7:51.

"That's what she said" joke as part of his acceptance. Jim and Pam heap extra praise onto Dwight, cognizant of how maniacally jealous it is making Michael. Unable to bear the sight of Dwight getting credit for something he has done, Michael bursts into the meeting Dwight and David are having with the marketing department. Michael explains that he asked Dwight to take the fall for the idea when it seemed like there would be negative consequences. After being pushed on the matter, Dwight finally admits, "Yes, it's Michael's idea that he forced on me on threat of death!"[18] Michael's response is a loud and triumphant, "Thank you!"[19] When David Wallace, the confused corporate representative, does not understand what has just happened, Michael admits, "Well, David, I will be honest with you. I do want the credit without any of the blame."[20]

Like Willy, Michael Scott is willfully blind. When he hears Jim talk about explaining the situation to corporate headquarters, he is only willing to see it as a golden ticket idea to get him out of trouble. He sees it as a sign of support. When Jim contradicts him, Michael accuses him of being greedy and petty to impress Pam. Michael is also willfully blind when Dwight exaggeratedly admits that Michael threatened his life. All Michael hears is an admission that it was his idea. Michael turns his face toward the warm glow of praise and turns a blind eye to what he has done, how he has put the branch and company in jeopardy, and how he has harmed others.

Michael and Willy are both willfully blind. Both are relatively powerful men who use their power to prop themselves up. They want the power and the praise, and they try to maneuver the people around them into only seeing what they want to see. Willy's family, with the exception of Biff, seems willing to go along with Willy's false ideas. The people in the Scranton branch of Dunder Mifflin seem to take for granted that being willfully blind is how Michael manages the branch and lives his life.

Death of a Salesman shows the tragic consequences of willful blindness. It is a tragedy not only because Willy ends up dead, and not only because his willful blindness impoverishes them, but because it has such painful effects on the entire family. Willy's wife, Linda, and his son, Happy, have grown so accustomed to the dishonesty that they willingly support it. When Biff tries to live truthfully and tries to genuinely connect with his father, Willy's willful blindness makes truth and connection impossible.

18. Einhorn, *Office*, 18:44–18:49.
19. Einhorn, *Office*, 18:50.
20. Einhorn, *Office*, 18:56–19:01.

Willful blindness not only disconnects people from the truth, but it disconnects them from others. *The Office* shows a humorous lack of consequences for willful blindness. No one ends up dead, and everyone is in about the same place at the end of the episode as they were at the beginning. Michael believes himself to be a good boss and a visionary manager, Dwight gets a moment in the sun, and everyone still has a job tomorrow.

Perhaps *The Office*'s humorous representation of willful blindness is just meant to be delightful. Perhaps we just enjoy spending time with these people, and we see the humorous extremes to which the willfully blind like Michael Scott might go. Perhaps the show's laughter is just about delight. But many people comment that they know people in their jobs or in their lives who are like Michael Scott.

Francis Hutcheson and the Edged Tool That Is Ridicule

This similarity to real life brings us to an eighteenth-century Scottish thinker's ideas about what he calls "ridicule." In 1725, Francis Hutcheson wrote three short essays about laughter. Hutcheson is an early voice for what is called the Incongruity Theory of Laughter. His idea is that what causes laughter is a "bringing together of images which have contrary additional ideas as well as some resemblance in the principle idea."[21] Laughter comes from blending contradictory ideas or elements. He elaborates that the "contrast between ideas of grandeur, dignity, sanctity, perfection, and ideas of meanness, baseness, profanity, seems to be the very spirit of burlesque; and the greatest part of our raillery and jest is founded upon it."[22] Combining high ideals like grandeur and dignity with their opposites like baseness and profanity is, for Hutcheson, what so often makes us laugh.

The "Golden Ticket" episode demonstrates such a combination. What we expect from leaders is wisdom, integrity, support for employees, and dedication to making their cause or business successful. At the start of the episode, Michael tries to convey his leadership skills. He introduces his promotional idea with the enthusiasm of Willy Wonka. When his plans fail miserably, what we expect is a leader who will honestly take responsibility, try to find the best solution, and help employees through the crisis. The episode brings together those expectations with contradictory additional ideas, specifically Michael's efforts to avoid responsibility, to shift the blame

21. Hutcheson, "Reflections upon Laughter," 32.
22. Hutcheson, "Reflections upon Laughter," 32.

to the employees, and to weasel out of the mess he's made. The grandeur and dignity Michael might try to convey are combined with their opposites by way of his pettiness and jealousy. Some of our laughter at the show comes from how contradictory elements humorously come together in the person of Michael Scott.

There is another important point that Hutcheson makes that gets us back to Michael Scott and Willy Loman. As a preface to his third essay, Hutcheson quotes Horace's idea that "joking often cuts through great obstacles better and more forcefully than being serious would."[23] Hutcheson's third essay is about how laughter, and specifically ridicule, can be a useful tool in bringing people to the truth. Hutcheson puts forward that ridicule can act like a pin or a knife, popping or lancing something that has gotten out of hand or out of proportion. He says that when something gets out of hand, or "when any object either good or evil is aggravated and increased by the violence of our passions, or an enthusiastic admiration, or fear,"[24] then the best remedy is ridicule. Hutcheson continues: "The application of ridicule is the readiest way to bring down our high imagination to a conformity to the real moment or importance of the affair."[25] Not only can ridicule lance an overinflated passion, admiration, or fear, but it can also return the mind back to reality. As Hutcheson puts it, "ridicule gives our minds as it were a bend to the contrary side; so that upon reflection they may be more capable of settling in a just conformity to nature."[26] In fact, you may have done this very thing. If you have ever had someone who is very passionate about a plan or belief or idea, and if you have seen how they have gotten carried away by that thing, you may have said this: "So how's that working out for you?" This simple, joking, and at least slightly ridiculing comment is usually meant to point out this error. It is meant to bring them back to reality. It is meant to bring them back to a more reasonable frame of mind, or, as Hutcheson would put it, bring them back to "a just conformity to nature."

The application of ridicule is, for Hutcheson, sometimes more effective than a serious approach. Still, Hutcheson recognizes that this is not always the case. Sometimes the laughter is not good-natured or the person on the other end does not take it as such. Some people are more than happy to keep their overinflated passions, admirations, or fears. They resent

23. Hutcheson, "Reflections upon Laughter," 35.
24. Hutcheson, "Reflections upon Laughter," 36.
25. Hutcheson, "Reflections upon Laughter," 36.
26. Hutcheson, "Reflections upon Laughter," 36–37.

people coming along with ridicule's pin or knife. Hutcheson recognizes this when he says, "Ridicule, like other edged tools, may do good in a wise man's hands, though fools may cut their fingers with it, or it be injurious to an unwary bystander."[27]

There is an interesting example of good-natured laughter or ridicule being used to pop inflated passions and bring someone back to a "just conformity to nature." In a short film by The School of Life dealing with humour in relationships, they examine Margaret Thatcher's reflections on how she responded to the television show *Spitting Image*.[28] The show exaggerated Thatcher's impatient authoritarianism and made her look like a psychopath. When Thatcher watched the show, she both chuckled at its humorous depiction of her and saw how the show's exaggerations revealed something truthful about her. Ridicule popped her overinflated impatience and authoritarianism, gave her mind a bend to a contrary or different side, and brought her back to a healthy approach and "just conformity to nature."

Thatcher's response to *Spitting Image* shows how ridicule can do good in a wise person's hands and when someone is willing to accept laughter's correction. Perhaps you have watched Michael Scott, reflected on some of your own tendencies or flaws or overinflated passions, and tried to learn from it. Perhaps you have caught yourself speaking or acting like Michael Scott, and this has at least made you pause, if not correct your course. But if you happen to have a boss who too often acts like Michael Scott, you will most likely seriously cut your fingers if you try to use ridicule to correct that boss. In addition, I cannot imagine Willy Loman being willing to accept even the best-natured ridicule that might be intended to bring him out of his willful blindness. Willy would probably feel picked on. And that is the thing about willful blindness—some people choose it so strongly, find it such a useful defense, and use it so effectively to fend off reality, that it is difficult to imagine ridicule's punchlines punching through such a barrier. But perhaps the wisest and funniest among us could, occasionally, do just that.

This entire "Maybe" section is about laughter that may or may not help people live better. In Hutcheson's optimistic view, ridicule is the good-natured joking that brings us back in line or brings us back to our senses. Laughter can invite us to reexamine our passions, values, and assumptions. The humorous lists found in *A Confederacy of Dunces*, *Dr. Strangelove*, and Borges's essay invite such reevaluation. Carnival laughter also does what

27. Hutcheson, "Reflections upon Laughter," 39.
28. The School of Life, "Humour in Relationships."

ridicule can do—invite error detection and reevaluation. In the carnival, you are free, as Malcolm says, "to let go and really see what you're capable of creating without worrying what anyone else thinks." You are free to play with values and virtues and taboos. You are free to insult and offend authorities. The carnival is a place to see things differently and to potentially see them better. Carnival freedom and insight isn't just found at Burning Man or the Feast of Fools. Paul Beatty's *The Sellout* places the reader in a mental space where that reader is free to play with and question values and taboos found in the official world and our everyday lives. Plays, novels, movies, television shows, and other forms of art provide a place that is apart from one's regular life or one's first life. They often use humor to invite reevaluation.

And this brings up this section's final dilemma. The carnival is different from the official, from one's everyday life. It is separate. That separation causes an interesting problem. First, sometimes the carnival is not far enough from the official world. Authorities in the official world don't like being insulted or mocked. They rarely respect how the carnival is different from the official world, so they will often do all they can to police or censor it. As discussed earlier in this section, it is difficult to respect the carnival and the official for what they provide and how they might complement one another. But there is another side to that distance. Since the carnival is not one's everyday life, is not real life, can it really have an impact? Do the freedom and error detection that the carnival invites actually lead to any real-world improvements? In other words, is anyone really better off after watching Michael Scott or Malcolm or Hal or Lois or Major Kong or Ignatius or Bonbon? Do audiences actually use laughter's delight to detect and then correct errors? It seems like the most optimistic answer has to be "maybe."

Yes

CHAPTER 9

Sigmund Freud and Brené Brown in *Zombieland*

I AM WRITING THIS chapter on my laptop in my house on Monday, March 23rd, 2020. There is a sort of zombie apocalypse happening right now with the coronavirus. I'm writing at home to do my part for social distancing and sheltering-in-place. The stock market has gone down from almost 30,000 to around 18,000. School and university classes have moved online, sports are suspended, and stores are either closed or scary. I would be writing the early drafts of this, like I normally do, on toilet paper, but toilet paper is such a precious commodity now that you can trade three pristine packs of Charmin for a brand-new Kia Sorento. It is a crazy time. It is, however, an excellent time to imagine Sigmund Freud and Brené Brown wandering through Zombieland.

Freud

I've been thinking about going on social media and posting this joke: A criminal is brought to the gallows on a Monday. Nearby are a handful of somber onlookers. The official who is about to hang the criminal asks if he has any last words. After a long pause, the criminal states blandly, "What a way to start my week!" Okay, so that is not a great joke, and I probably won't post it, not only because it is not that funny but because this is still a pretty dark, serious time.

Yes

The joke about the criminal hanged on a Monday is an adaptation of a joke Freud uses in his 1928 essay "Humour."[1] When I teach my college seminar on laughter, I tell the students that one way to understand any thinker's ideas about laughter is to look for that person's sample joke or anecdote. I tell them to work back from that example to see how the thinker explains why we laugh at it. This works well with Freud because his essay seems like an explanation of that joke.

What Freud says about the joke is that the man telling the joke uses the joke as a defense mechanism. The moment that he is about to die is of course very stressful and traumatic. Instead of being overwhelmed by the situation, the man seems to brush it all off with a joke. Freud's idea is that there are three elements behind everything people do. Everyone has inner drives that Freud calls the id. Everyone also has the self that Freud associates with language and logic. Freud calls this self the ego. This is the part of you that says, "I am." The third part is like an internal parent. This is the part that keeps the ego from going along with whatever the id might want. This third part, since it is outside, over, and in some ways superior to the ego, is called the superego.

So what is the joke-teller trying to defend himself against and how does he do it? For Freud, the joke-teller is defending himself against suffering. The way that the joke-teller defends himself against suffering is by a shift in focus off of the ego. The joke allows him to stop seeing what is happening through his ego, through the part that soon will die, and instead to see what is happening to him from the point-of-view of the superego. Since the superego is above and outside of the ego, the joke's shift in focus allows the criminal to escape suffering. When the man's death is viewed from the outside and superior perspective of the superego, what is happening to the ego seems trivial and laughable.

Freud describes how the humorous shifting of focus from the vulnerable ego to the invulnerable superego helps that ego deal with trauma. Freud also describes how making a joke in the face of trauma can affect bystanders. Freud pictures a somber bystander watching the criminal marched to the gallows. That bystander would naturally anticipate serious last words. The bystander is ready to feel empathy, sorrow, grief, or contempt for the criminal. What the bystander gets instead is a joke. This sudden reversal of what the bystander expects could cause the bystander to laugh out loud. Freud puts forward the idea that the bystander had expected to connect

---

1. Freud, "Humour."

with the pain, fear, horror, or despair that the criminal would express. But the bystander does not have those feelings because what the criminal gave instead was a joke. In fact, the joke invites the bystander to also shift the focus from vulnerable egos to invulnerable superegos. The joke invites the bystander to escape suffering or at least the unwanted feelings that were anticipated. The joke lifts the bystander and the criminal so that both can look down on temporary and trivial egos from superego heights.

Freud in *Zombieland*

Zombieland begins with images of Washington DC, a smoldering Capitol building, an overturned Secret Service vehicle, and a Jimi Hendrix-like guitar rendition of the "Star-Spangled Banner." In a voiceover, a narrator explains that you cannot have a country without people, and there are no longer any people, just zombies. After a gruesome scene of a zombie attack, the camera then zooms out very, very quickly, revealing a chaotic, blistering, and fiery planet. We see the entire burning world from above.

From this the narrator continues, posing this question in a deadpan way: "And why am I alive when everyone around me has turned to meat? It's because of my list of rules."[2] At this point the globe spins to reveal a sports stadium where a fat guy runs to escape a zombie. The narrator explains, "Rule number one for surviving Zombieland . . . Cardio. When the virus struck, for obvious reasons, the first ones to go were the fatties. Poor fat bastard!"[3] The next images are of cars crashing and people running in chaos. The narrator continues, "But as the infection spread and the chaos grew, it wasn't enough just being fast on your feet; you had to get a gun and learn how to use it. Which leads me to my second rule: The Double Tap."[4] We see a woman shooting and narrowly escaping a zombie police officer. The voiceover continues, "In those moments when you're not sure that the 'undead' are really 'dead dead,' don't get all stingy with your bullets."[5] Just when it appears that the woman who shot the zombie is safe, the merely wounded zombie attacks that woman, grabbing her by the leg. She is then overwhelmed by other zombies. The voiceover explains, "I mean one more

---

2. Fleischer, *Zombieland*, 1:12–1:18.
3. Fleischer, *Zombieland*, 1:19–1:36.
4. Fleischer, *Zombieland*, 1:38–1:51.
5. Fleischer, *Zombieland*, 1:53–1:58.

clean shot to the head, and this lady could have avoided becoming a human Happy Meal. Woulda, coulda, shoulda!"[6] These first scenes in the movie do a couple of things. They set the movie's humorous tone. Part of the way this is done is just what Freud describes. We see the Earth from above and at a distance. We see, again from above, the unfortunate fat man being chased and caught in a stadium. We see the woman who believes she has gotten away but is sadly mistaken. The narrator's deadpan voice contrasts sharply with the tragedy we are witnessing. As Freud explains, the accent has moved from the individuals, from the vulnerable egos that we see suffering. That accent is placed on something above and outside of those egos. That is where we are, and that outside, superior view is that of a superego. From the point-of-view of the superego, what happens to egos is trivial and laughable. They are "poor fat bastards" and "human Happy Meals."

In the terror of the zombie apocalypse, jokes like these create emotional distance. The narrator makes jokes to both shift the focus toward the superego and to look past the suffering he sees all around him. Jokes like these come up all through the movie. Partway through the movie, there is a discussion about the "Zombie Kill of the Week." Zombie killing has become a reality game show. When the narrator claims that the award goes to a prim, church-going woman who killed a zombie by dropping a piano on him, the narrator jokes that the zombie became a "poor, flat bastard."[7] Toward the end of the movie, the narrator accidently shoots Bill Murray. Instead of getting upset, Murray responds, "Is that how you say hello where you come from?"[8] Murray is then asked if he has any regrets. He pauses for a long, thoughtful moment, and then responds, "*Garfield*, maybe."[9] This joke is actually a sort of updated, funnier version of the one Freud used. Right when we expect Murray might say something somber or deeply meaningful, he mentions a regrettable role in a regrettable movie. All of these jokes reinforce emotional distance between characters. They invite audiences to look at what is happening from a similar safe emotional distance.

An important element of these scenes that shows the shift from the ego to the superego is the narrator's rules. These rules create a strong link between the ego and superego, since the superego is associated with parents.

6. Fleischer, *Zombieland*, 1:59–2:09.

7. Fleischer, *Zombieland*, 42:05.

8. Fleischer, *Zombieland*, 53:52–53:55.

9. Fleischer, *Zombieland*, 54:39–54:40.

Parents create and enforce rules, and the superego's rules keep the ego and the id in check and under control. Rules apply beyond one ego and one moment, stretching over everyone and through the past, present, and future. *Zombieland*'s narrator finds order, control, and safety in the superego as expressed in his survival rules. In addition, the rules help the narrator avoid risky situations. When the narrator introduces his third rule he says, "When you are at your most vulnerable, somehow [the zombies] can just smell it. Don't let them catch you with your pants down. Rule #3: 'Beware of Bathrooms.'"[10] Bathrooms are risky because there you can figuratively and literally be caught unprepared and with your pants down.

There is one rule that brings many of these elements together. That is Rule #7: Travel Light. When the narrator introduces this rule, he says, "And I don't mean just luggage."[11] Traveling light means avoiding the weight of human relationships and connections. The narrator attributes part of his success as a survivor to being a loner. Even when the narrator meets others and spends time with them, they do not refer to each other by their first names. When the narrator, Columbus, meets another human, that man calls himself Tallahassee. Tallahassee goes so far as to state that using the names of where people are from helps them avoid getting too comfortable with each other.

The best way to be comfortable in Zombieland is to be above it, aloof, and as emotionally distant as possible. This is done by not using people's proper names but only names of the places where they come from. This is done by traveling light and avoiding physical and emotional baggage. This is done by making jokes at the expense of others, by laughing at suffering as if it will not happen to you. This is done by shifting the focus off of yourself and onto something that is above you, something that is like a parent. The connection with this parent is stronger by following rules as if they came from that parent. Those rules will keep you safe. All of this will keep you from suffering, from the trauma, chaos, and despair all around you. That is how you survive Zombieland.

Brené Brown

If *Zombieland* were 88 minutes of jokes about the suffering of poor fat and flat bastards, it would get old rather quickly. It would end up being a gory,

10. Fleischer, *Zombieland*, 2:12–2:30.

11. Fleischer, *Zombieland*, 7:17–7:21.

bloody, zombie version of *America's Funniest Home Videos*. It would also have a significant hole in the middle. Brené Brown helps us identify that hole.

Freud's view of laughter is that it creates distance that helps the ego avoid suffering. But Brown has a very different view about human connection and about what causes suffering. Brown firmly states that "the surest thing I took away from my PSW, MSW, and PhD in social work is this: connection is why we are here. We are hardwired to connect with others, it's what gives purpose and meaning to our lives, and without it there is suffering."[12] Where emotional distance and invulnerability keep an ego safe from suffering in Freud's view, it is their opposites, connection and vulnerability, that, for Brown, bring purpose and meaning to one's life. What causes suffering in Brown's view are the very things that for Freud prevent suffering and visa versa.

Brown recognizes that connection and vulnerability are risky. She defines vulnerability as "uncertainty, risk, and emotional exposure."[13] She talks about one of the riskiest forms of vulnerability—love. Talking about love's risks, she says,

> Waking up every day and loving someone who may or may not love us back, whose safety we can't ensure, who may stay in our lives or may leave without a moment's notice, who may be loyal to the day they die or betray us tomorrow—that's vulnerability. Love is uncertain. It's incredibly risky. And loving someone leaves us emotionally exposed. Yes, it's scary, and yes, we're open to being hurt, but can you imagine your life without loving or being loved?[14]

This quote gets us to the heart of *Zombieland*. The movie isn't really about zombies or coronavirus or some outside threat. The movie is about choosing to love or not in the face of fear. It is about taking the risks of connecting with others, reaching out to them, and making yourself vulnerable. It is about what that means, how it is risky, how it causes pain, and how it might bring joy. For Brown, humans are wired for connection, and connection requires vulnerability. What this also means, for Brown, is that "vulnerability is the birthplace of love, belonging, joy, courage, empathy, and creativity. It is the source of hope, empathy, accountability, and

12. Brown, *Daring Greatly*, 8.
13. Brown, *Daring Greatly*, 34.
14. Brown, *Daring Greatly*, 34.

authenticity."[15] One gets to a meaningful life, a life with depth and purpose, only by taking the path of vulnerability.

Brown in Zombieland

Columbus, *Zombieland*'s narrator and central character, shows connection and vulnerability's risks and rewards. Columbus has three very painful experiences. Those experiences illustrate the risks inherent in vulnerability. The first is his experience with the attractive young woman next door. As she is in room 406, we only know her as 406. She comes to Columbus's room after being attacked by what she describes as a homeless man. Columbus takes her in, comforts her like a true gentleman—with Code Red Mountain Dew and a Ziploc bag of Golden Grahams—and offers her the safety of the shoulder where she can rest her tired and beautiful head. Unfortunately, she soon becomes a maniacal, bloodthirsty zombie. You would think that an experience like this might give a young man second thoughts, but Columbus still wants what he has always wanted—to find a girl, fall in love, and bring her home to meet the folks. He wants connection and closeness. He wants to "brush a girl's hair over her ear."[16] In fact, when he first meets Wichita, he comments that she might be someone to bring home to the folks and "someone's ear was in danger of having hair brushed over it."[17]

Columbus's initial experience with Wichita and her sister Little Rock turns out to be almost as painful as his experience with 406. The sisters take advantage of Columbus's and Tallahassee's sensitivity and trust. Vulnerability is met with indifference and betrayal. For a second time vulnerability's risks have produced painful outcomes for Columbus. When the four get back together, finally reach an unsteady truce, and end up in Bill Murray's mansion, the possibility of healthy and satisfying connection with Wichita presents itself for Columbus. But for the third time, her almost immediate abandonment leaves him with pain and loneliness.

At this point, Columbus has already started to break his rules. Instead of traveling lightly by setting off on his own or perhaps tagging along with Tallahassee to Mexico, Columbus chooses to pursue Wichita. When he finds her and her sister in danger at the amusement park, we reach the movie's emotional climax. This is the point at which Columbus

15. Brown, *Daring Greatly*, 34.
16. Fleischer, *Zombieland*, 16:07–16:09.
17. Fleischer, *Zombieland*, 23:50–23:53.

must determine whether the risks of vulnerability are worth its possible rewards. As Columbus makes his way to the Blast Off ride where the sisters are trapped, he must decide if he will risk his life to save the girls. The movie makes this a decision between keeping or breaking Rule #17: "Don't be a Hero." He is in fact taking several risks. He risks losing his life in the effort to save the girls. He takes a risk by breaking the very rules he believes have kept him safe and alive. He cannot know beforehand how his act of heroism and vulnerability will turn out even if he is successful. Wichita has twice betrayed and abandoned him, so even if he were successful in rescuing her, the odds don't seem to be that great that she would reach back, connect back, or reciprocate his connection-making gesture. When Columbus succeeds in saving the girls, and, at the movie's most intimate moment, when Columbus and Wichita finally embrace, she whispers the most vulnerable and intimate thing she could give—her name. Wichita returns Columbus's vulnerable risk-taking, and both enjoy a rewarding moment of connection.

Columbus's risky efforts to save Wichita and Little Rock show him moving from emotional distance to emotional connection. He rejects the safety his rules offered him. At the moment of crisis, Columbus could have remembered the girls' betrayals, held to his rules, looked up at them, and said, "Poor trapped bastards." Not only does he not do that, but there is more going on in this scene. What we find in this moment is Columbus rejecting a certain form of laughter. What initially gets in the way of helping the girls is not just his rule, "Don't Be a Hero." Columbus also faces a lifelong fear—clowns. And the clown he faces isn't just any clown, this is a zombie clown. On one level, this clown embodies his many fears that he must overcome in order to connect with someone who has come to mean a lot to him. On another level, the zombie clown represents Freud's ideas about laughter. Freudian laughter is a defense mechanism against fear, suffering, and reality. Freudian laughter transports someone out of the world of vulnerable humans, lifting the joke-teller to a place of comfort, security, and emotional distance. A zombie clown is an excellent symbol for Freudian laughter, since this is laughter that avoids the risks and rewards of suffering, of being vulnerable, and of being human. Zombie clowns are not alive to the risks and realities of others. A zombie clown is an undead-but-still-rather-dead humor-maker. It does not care about other people or other egos. In fact, it would just feed off of them. When Columbus humorously defeats the zombie clown, he symbolically rejects the emotionally distant and defensive laughter it represents.

Given what is stated so far, especially about Columbus's metaphorical defeat of defense-mechanism humor, it may seem as if connection and vulnerability are incompatible with humor. Humor, at least Freudian defense-mechanism humor, rejects vulnerability and connection. But Freud's view does not account for all humorous expression. In fact, there are two moments where humor seems to recognize and even honor vulnerability. Columbus first meets Tallahassee on a wreckage-strewn highway. They face off, each with his gun aimed at the other. This standoff lasts for a few awkwardly amusing moments until Columbus hesitantly lowers his gun and raises his thumb. This gesture is humorously incongruous given that both seemed like they might kill each other. The hitchhiking gesture is a surrender flag, a petition for help, and an offer of companionship. This is an important first moment when Columbus demonstrates his willingness to take the risk of vulnerability, a risk that is humorously incongruent given the traumatic circumstances.

A more important moment that combines humor and vulnerability comes at the end of the movie. After Columbus and Tallahassee have helped the sisters defeat the amusement park zombies, the sisters seem to be driving off in the SUV. The men start to chase after them, disappointed that they have been abandoned and betrayed yet again. The vehicle then suddenly stops, and Wichita looks out of the window at them with a smile. Relieved, Tallahassee and Columbus move to the SUV, and Columbus quips, "That's very funny."[18] No, it is not very funny, but the incident brings back past betrayals. The girls have done that very thing to them twice already. This is a sudden reversal, and it brings a sudden relief that no, the sisters will not leave them again. In that respect, the quick joke recognizes vulnerability, it reverses the painful experiences of the past, and it offers a pleasant surprise in the present. It is a small but significant moment that humorously honors vulnerability and connection.

Many of the humorous elements and jokes at the beginning of *Zombieland* match up with Freud's ideas about humor as a defense mechanism. Those jokes invite emotional distance as we laugh at poor fat bastards, poor flat bastards, and human happy meals. Columbus survives because of rules that offer some of the same things that parental rules give children—security, order, and protection. Characters and audiences look down on the chaos and the suffering of others as trivial, laughable matters. But the movie soon mixes that emotional distance with emotional connection. Characters

18. Fleischer, *Zombieland*, 1:22:20.

start to connect, or at least attempt to connect, with others, and audiences connect with characters. In the end the movie is about the advantages and the limitations of emotional distance, of emotionally distant laughter, and the risks and rewards of vulnerability and connection. The movie shifts from humor as a defense mechanism to humor that honors connection. As it moves from a distant, zombielike detachment to human engagement, what you are left with is a point that is one of Columbus's last statements: "Without other people, well, you might as well be a zombie."[19]

19. Fleischer, *Zombieland*, 1:22:08–1:22:12.

CHAPTER 10

The Dad Jokes Chapter with a Secret at the End

IT MIGHT GO SOMETHING like this—an unsuspecting six-year-old sees her father making a snack in the kitchen and asks, "Can you make me a sandwich?" The father points at the child, makes an abracadabra gesture, and proclaims, "You are a sandwich!" Moments before this, she may have innocently said, "I'm hungry," to which that same father replied, "Hi hungry, I'm Dad."

Dad jokes. This chapter is about dad jokes, but before that, we start with this question: Why don't we have "mom jokes?" Moms are just as intelligent, creative, witty, and humorous as dads. Why aren't "mom jokes" a thing? And while we're asking questions, why, in the name of all that is holy, do dads continue to tell dad jokes when they are no longer funny to anyone else? Oh, and finally, there is a secret at the end of this chapter.

Guido Woos Dora

When a young woman falls into a man's arms, he says, "What a place here! It's beautiful! Pigeons fly, women fall from the sky. I'm moving here!"[1] He says this to a lovely woman who has just fallen from the sky. Okay, she fell from a loft while trying to burn out some wasps. He happened to be right under the loft and caught her. He's obviously quite smitten with her. Even as he's leaving, he slips a stick behind his back and uses it to lift his hat. For a moment it looks a bit magical, and then it looks funny and silly.

---

1. Benigni, *Life Is Beautiful*, 4:43–4:48.

When he runs into her again, he literally runs into her. He is on a bike, turns a corner, loses control of the bike, and falls into her. Where she had fallen on him previously, now he falls on her. Again, both are unharmed. He smiles and wonders aloud if they will ever bump into each other standing up. Sometime later he sees her walking in a plaza with a friend. He hides behind his friend to theatrically jump out and say hello. She notes that he always seems to just suddenly show up, so he suggests that they meet up on purpose, perhaps for dinner that night. With a smile she tells him that she prefers running into him suddenly. At this point the man, Guido, does not know that Dora is in a serious romantic relationship. He just knows how much he likes her.

He finds out that her name is Dora and that she works with school children. She's probably a teacher. Guido meets a school inspector who will be visiting Dora's school the next morning. Guido decides to show up at the school and impersonate the inspector. He arrives with an official sash over his shoulder. Dora is again surprised to see him. The principal introduces Guido to the other teachers, and now he must improvise some questions that sound like what an inspector might ask. Humorously, they are just the sort of empty, bureaucratic questions one would expect: How long have you taught here? Are you up on this or that curriculum? Are you familiar with a recent education memo? When he gets to Dora, he relaxes and asks her what she's doing on Sunday. Once he finds out that she's going to an Offenbach opera, he prepares to leave. The principal insists that he stay so he can lecture on the superiority of the Italian race. Pushed into this service, he makes a seemingly serious show of the request, but he sprinkles it with phrases like "our racist Italian scientists."[2] He then offers a ridiculous demonstration of how he is part of the superior race because of his perfect earlobes. His presentation ends with him making a silly dance but not before we see him in his shirt and boxers showing off his perfect Aryan belly button. An amused Dora smiles her approval. When the real inspector arrives, Guido makes his escape out a window, showing off that belly button one more time, and promising Dora he'll see her at the theater.

When Guido encounters Dora again, he accuses her of following him. He says that when he just happens to stop, she falls into his arms. He falls off his bike and ends up in her arms. He goes to inspect a school, and there she is again. She even follows him into his dreams. He mock requests that she leave him alone, noting that she must really have a crush on him. Of

2. Benigni, *Life Is Beautiful*, 23:18.

course all of that is not exactly true, but given the wide and warm smile on her face, he may be correct that she has something for him.

Guido and Dora's is a lovely little story, and we'll return to it later. What you see in Guido is something you have probably seen very often—a man using humor to try to woo a woman, or at least to try to gauge her interest in him. This is also just the sort of thing that social scientists, people who cannot leave well enough alone, feel the need to analyze. Two such social scientists are Christopher Wilbur and Lorna Campbell. Wilbur and Campbell set up three studies to see how men and women use humor to initiate romantic relationships. For the first study, they had almost 500 college students respond to a questionnaire. Some of the questions were about expressing humor appreciation. A humor appreciation item would be something like "I would act amused by his/her jokes" or "I would tell him/her that he/she was funny."[3] Some of the items were about humor production, such as "I would tell some funny stories" or "I would make witty remarks."[4] The last questions were about humor evaluation: "I would try to determine if his/her jokes seem to flow spontaneously rather than being forced" or "I would attempt to evaluate how naturally amusing he/she is."[5] When researchers looked at the results of this study, they found that men were inclined to be humor-producers. Women scored higher in humor evaluation and humor appreciation.

Wilbur and Campbell's second study examined dating profiles. Here again they found that men were humor-producers, whereas women were more likely to request humorous production. Men were socialized to be seen as humorous, and women were socialized to evaluate and desire humorous men. In their last study, they wanted to look at humor production. They wanted to see if there was a connection between someone making you laugh and you being romantically interested in them. They had men and women evaluate dating profiles they had created. They found that when women found the profiles humorous, they were more romantically interested. In contrast, the humorousness of the profile did not make men more romantically interested. Wilbur and Campbell's research gives solid evidence for this idea: men are socialized to be humor-producers and women are socialized to be humor-appreciators. Guido is a humor-producer, and Dora is attracted to him in part because of his humor production.

3. Wilbur and Campbell, "Humor in Romantic Contexts," 921.

4. Wilbur and Campbell, "Humor in Romantic Contexts," 921.

5. Wilbur and Campbell, "Humor in Romantic Contexts," 921.

Tiffany Haddish

Not many fifteen-year-old African-American girls in foster care ever have
to convince a judge that one day they will be successful comedians. Had
you asked me before I read Tiffany Haddish's memoir, *The Last Black Unicorn*, I would have guessed that total was zero. The story goes like this—the
young Haddish was living in Southern California. She was in foster care,
and her social worker gave her two options—psychiatric therapy or go to
the Laugh Factory Comedy Camp. Because she was afraid of medication,
Haddish didn't want anything to do with psychiatric therapy. She chose
Laugh Factory Comedy Camp, and that camp turned out to be perfect for
the young Haddish. She met comics like Dane Cook, Chris Spencer, and
the Wayans brothers. She learned how comedy can be like music from
Quincy Jones. From none other than Richard Pryor she learned the value
of enjoying herself as a comic. But what she valued the most at that time
was that she felt safe at the camp. She had seen a lot of neglect and abuse in
her short fifteen years. Comedy camp was a sanctuary.

During that time, a television crew came and did a story about Haddish. She was excited about being on the news, but the problem was getting permission. Since the state of California had to give permission for
the television story to run, Haddish had to take public transportation to
family court to get that permission. Not only was the court far, but the first
day that she went she could not get the judge to review her case. It took a
second visit for a judge to finally pay any attention to her. The judge didn't
understand why she needed to be on the news, so she told him that she was
at the Laugh Factory Comedy Camp and that she was going to "be a world-
famous comedian."[6] It took some convincing, but she persuaded the judge
to sign off on the permission.

This story is important to Haddish because it came back to her many
years later. Over time she had lost sight of her dream of being a world-
famous comedian. After some serious emotional and physical trauma, she
came back to how comedy was what she was supposed to do. She started
doing open-mic shows and developed her skills. Eventually she was asked
to do a show, but that performance was a catastrophe. It went so poorly
that she second-guessed her decision. What got her through that setback
was Haddish's memory of telling the judge that someday she'd be a world-
famous comedian. It also helped that, in spite of bombing, she got paid.

6. Haddish, *Last Black Unicorn*, 32.

When Haddish talks about this time and her decision to pursue comedy in her memoir, she explores some of the joy comedy brings her. She says she feels that on stage, telling jokes, is where she's supposed to be. She admits how mentally demanding the work is. She writes about how much she likes the adrenaline rush and how "nothing else makes my mind work so fast and so hard."[7] She works so hard precisely because of the risks inherent in not knowing if you are going to make people laugh or not. She also explores the power she feels as a comedian. She says "the power that comes with it is intoxicating."[8] On stage she has power she does not have elsewhere, and it is there, in spite of hard work and risks, that she feels brave.

Haddish's experiences as a comic tell us a few things about dad jokes. First, they show that women are just as intelligent, talented, and funny as men. Dad jokes are not a thing because dads are smarter or funnier. In fact, with as lame as many dad jokes tend to be, they would seem to call into question inherent male intellect much more than promote it! Moms can be as funny as dads. The second idea is that telling jokes is risky, but it can make the teller feel brave and powerful. Haddish's risks and feeling of power are much greater than a typical dad in a kitchen who is magically turning his daughter into a sandwich, but even that dad can feel powerful when he makes her laugh. Dads begin to feel this power when their children are very, very small by playing peek-a-boo or giving raspberries. They feel it with the physical humor that little kids like and then with the classic dad wordplay that slightly older children can enjoy.

The power dads feel making their children laugh is, as Haddish described, intoxicating. It is joyous and euphoric. It is a way for dads to bond with their children. It also continues what men had been socialized to do to get here in the first place. Men are socialized to use humor, like Guido, to woo a partner. After they get that partner, while the jokes may or may not stop, a dad brings those same skills to bond with their children. Dad jokes follow from how men are socialized to be humor-producers.

Mateo and Adi

A seven-year-old girl, her father, and an anthropologist are in Marshall, Pennsylvania. The father, Mateo, speaks Spanish and some English, while the girl, Adi, and the anthropologist, Sarah, speak English and Spanish. As

7. Haddish, *Last Black Unicorn*, 143.
8. Haddish, *Last Black Unicorn*, 144.

they are talking, Adi is disturbed to know that if she and her father return to Mexico, they will not be able to return to Pennsylvania to see their anthropologist friend because of their undocumented status. Sarah explains that she could visit them, and when Adi seems perplexed, her father explains that Sarah can come and go across the border as she'd like. With a big sigh, Adi says in Spanish "I need papers."[9] Her father grabs a sheet of paper and responds, in Spanish, "Here you go."[10]

Mateo tells a dad joke, a rather simple play on words that is mildly humorous at best. But Sarah Gallo, the anthropologist who saw the exchange, notes that there is a lot more going on here. Gallo sees Mateo's joke as part of how this father uses humor to teach his daughter to deal with discrimination. Mateo's joke makes light of the papers. By turning the situation into a joke, he shows that the papers are only important because the powerful system surrounding them makes those papers important. Papers are what law enforcement use to target Mateo and his daughter. Papers make them strangers, people who do not belong here. Papers make them lesser and illegal. In addition, papers make a difference in their lives now and in the past, since for years the family was divided because of their lack of papers.

That seems like a lot to say about a dad joke. Does Adi get all of that stuff out of his joke? Gallo mentions other times when Mateo makes similar jokes. Those jokes make light of the difficult realities the family faces. One afternoon, when Mateo, Adi, and Sarah were out, Adi asked her father where he was going. When he replied, "Over there," she pressed him with "Where?"[11] To this second question, Mateo joked, "What are you, a police officer?"[12] Following along with the humorous hypothetical, Adi said, "Yes." Mateo then retorted, "Well I won't speak until I have my lawyer."[13] Adi rolled her eyes, shook her head, and proclaimed, "You don't have a lawyer anymore because I took her away. It's Sarah. She is my lawyer. Now who are you going to get? Do you know another *Americana* like Sarah?"[14] Mateo in mock resignation said, "No." Adi is clearly well acquainted with joking in this way. She naturally takes her part in this humorous version of a very serious and potentially very real situation.

9. Gallo, "Humor in Father-Daughter Immigration Narratives," 286.
10. Gallo, "Humor in Father-Daughter Immigration Narratives," 286.
11. Gallo, "Humor in Father-Daughter Immigration Narratives," 286.
12. Gallo, "Humor in Father-Daughter Immigration Narratives," 286.
13. Gallo, "Humor in Father-Daughter Immigration Narratives," 286.
14. Gallo, "Humor in Father-Daughter Immigration Narratives," 286.

Adi's jokes show that she knows about the risks that the family lives with. They also show that she is aware of realities that those with papers would not need to understand. She knows at least some of the basics of interacting with the police and finding help in the legal system. Mateo's jokes have rubbed off on Adi to the degree that she can take the role of the police. More importantly, Mateo's jokes use humor to teach her how to deal with such authorities.

And dealing with such authorities is something Adi faces. Gallo's article recounts an experience Adi and her father had three months later. While she was getting ready for school, Mateo was looking outside for her ride. He saw the police arrive and joked that it was immigration. When they knocked on the door, Adi acted as translator and go-between. Now she had to speak to the authorities she had playfully imitated. When they told her to open the door, what did she do? She did something the jokes had taught her to do—request papers. But here the papers are a search warrant. Since those officers didn't have those papers, they left. But about two hours later, another policeman came to their home. Adi again asked for his papers, but this time, the officer asked what was going on in the home. Mateo told Adi to follow up by asking the officer what he wanted. He said that he was looking for someone and told them to open the door or he'd force it open. Adi and Mateo opened the door, and the officer explained that he was there to see if they had any information about a suspected drug criminal. Mateo answered their questions. When the discussion was finished, the officer asked Adi why she wasn't in school. She replied that she was afraid that officers would come to take her father away.

Okay, nothing about this is funny. But there is something serious and important about how Mateo uses humor. Mateo uses jokes to humorously teach his daughter very important lessons about getting along in a dangerous world. His puns and his playacting teach her about power, documents, and how to use the tools at hand to deal with a difficult situation. Yes, Mateo tells dad jokes, jokes that are wordplay or only semi-humorous playacting. But Mateo's dad jokes playfully teach his daughter, in an amusing manner, important survival skills. Those jokes also strengthen the bond between father and daughter, connecting them through laughter and courage in the face of shared challenges.

Guido and Giosuè

It is some years later and the married Guido and Dora have a son, Giosuè. Approximately four years old, Giosuè accompanies his father as they drop Dora off at school and then walk past a café. The sign on the café's glass door says, "No Jews or Dogs."[15] Giosuè wants to go in and buy pastries for his mother, but his father quickly makes a joke about the pastries being artificial. After he reads the sign, Giosuè asks why Jews and dogs are not allowed into the café. Guido explains that the owners just happen to have a thing against Jews and dogs in their restaurant. Guido jokingly convinces his son that it is perfectly normal for some businesses to pose such restrictions. He tells his son that a nearby hardware store does not allow Spaniards or horses, and the local pharmacy prohibits Chinese people and kangaroos. Seemingly convinced, the son asks why the family's bookstore does not have similar restrictions. Guido takes this as a good idea, asking his son what animals they should prohibit. Giosuè says spiders. Guido agrees and adds that, in addition to spiders, they will also keep out any Visigoths who happen to want to shop there. Guido states with comic emphasis that tomorrow he will write the sign, "No Spiders or Visigoths."[16]

Guido does not tell jokes like Mateo. Mateo's dad jokes prepare his daughter to live and thrive in their difficult situation. Guido's jokes with Giosuè shield him from their situation. The Jewish Guido and his non-Jewish wife Dora in the movie *Life is Beautiful* live in Italy just before and during World War II. The first half of the movie shows how Guido met, wooed, and married Dora, while the second half focuses on how Guido tries to reunite with Dora while shielding their son from the horrors of a forced labor camp.

Guido and Giosuè are rounded up, put on a truck and then a train, and sent to the camp on what turns out to be Giosuè's birthday. Dora rushes to the station, realizes that her husband and son are being taken away, and gets on the train so as to not be separated from them. Guido does not want to tell Giosuè what is happening, so he makes jokes about how unpleasant the trip to the camp was and how they should take a nice bus home. Guido's next tactic is to tell his son that this is all part of an elaborate game. He ends up explaining a point system based on his son not crying, complaining, or

15. Benigni, *Life Is Beautiful*, 50:29.
16. Benigni, *Life Is Beautiful*, 51:10–51:14.

asking for his mother or more food. The rules of the game are ways Guido will help keep his son physically and emotionally safe.

One of the most humorous moments in the film comes when a burly and gruff German guard explains the camp rules. Guido steps forward when a request is made for someone who speaks German. Guido does not speak German. Guido "translates" the guard's harsh, dehumanizing, soul-crushing instructions into elements of the game Giosuè will be playing. One translation warns that it is easy to lose points for being hungry, and that the guard himself lost 40 points the previous day because he "absolutely had to have a jam sandwich."[17]

Guido adjusts the game as necessary to help his son survive. As the Allies move closer to the camp, Guido takes advantage of the time to try to get Dora and Giosuè out. He tells Giosuè that this is the final challenge, and that if he wins this final challenge, he will win the prize. He hides his son and goes to get Dora, but in the process, he is captured. A soldier leads him down an alley and guns him down. His son does as he is told, and in the movie's fanciful, delightful ending, Giosuè gets the promised prize and is reunited with his mother.

The fictional Guido's jokes shield his son and preserve his innocence. The real-life Mateo's humor instructs his daughter on how to face their shared painful, oppressive situation. When government officials first take Guido away, he looks back at his son with a comically broad smile and an exaggerated and silly walk. This same smile and exaggerated silly walk are also how he tells his son goodbye. Guido's jokes are exaggerated and silly, appropriate for a small child. Mateo's are subtle and subversive, appropriate for an older child. Finally, both fathers' dad jokes demonstrate the power and the courage that Tiffany Haddish describes.

The Secret

I'd love to meet Mateo and Guido someday. We could sit around and trade dad jokes. If our conversation went a little long, hopefully there'd be a kid who would say, "Dad, I wanna go home. I'm bored." We'd raise an eyebrow, and one would reply, "Hi bored, I'm Dad." In fact, when I told one of my students about this chapter, he said he had the best dad joke ever. Intrigued, of course, I said, "Okay, what is it." He explained that it is just one line: "Hi Sick-and-Tired-Taking-the-Kids-and-Never-Coming-Back, I'm Dad."

17. Benigni, *Life Is Beautiful*, 1:08:30–1:08:33.

Yes

This joke leads to this chapter's last question—Why do dads still tell dad jokes after kids and others no longer find them funny? Mateo strategically uses jokes. His jokes help Adi to not take the situation too seriously and not get too overwhelmed by it. His jokes teach her about power and the legal system. But will she still find them funny when she's eleven or thirteen or seventeen? What about when she's an adult? She probably will not, but there is a good chance that Mateo might very well keep telling them. Whenever she mentions needing papers, he might be ready to hand her a blank sheet of loose leaf. So why?

Some easy answers come to mind. Making people laugh can make you feel powerful. Perhaps dads still like the power that they feel. Now that those around Dad no longer find his jokes genuinely funny, they may merely groan or roll their eyes. But even if Dad makes them groan, it still gives him a slightly intoxicating jolt of power. It isn't abusive power. Well, it isn't too abusive. Or maybe dads still think they are funny. That could be remarkable self-deception. But I think there might be another reason. I think that some dads continue to tell some dad jokes to their children for this secret reason: Those dads miss their children. Dads miss the kids who were so delighted and impressed by a funny face, an exaggerated fall, or a silly pun. Dad jokes are a little time machine, a portal into the past allowing dads to be with who their children used to be. Dads are glad that they are older and have grown up, but perhaps some dad jokes reconnect dads with the people they loved and still love.

Chapter 11

Laughter that Melts Fear

Taking Swings

A LOUD, TINNY CLINK followed by two hard thuds. Another clink followed by a thud. Two clinks in quick succession and then three very loud thuds. Distant, muffled giggling. Signs of a gathering crowd. Police arrive. Law enforcement surveys the situation and quickly realizes that they have a problem. This is a problem not covered in their law enforcement handbook, and that is unusual, since this is a police state. You'd think they'd have a policy for everything.

The dilemma that these Serbian police face is who exactly to arrest. Once they get through the crowd, they realize what it was that brought those people together. It is the summer of 1999, and in the city square, police have found what caused the clinks, the thuds, the laughter, and the crowd. It is a large, empty oil drum that has been painted red. Taped to the drum is a picture of their boss, Serbian President Slobodan Milošević. A hole has been cut in the top of the drum with instructions that anyone who puts a coin in the slot can use the large stick to take a whack at the barrel. Citizens have assembled to pay for the chance to "pay" their respects, and even more people are watching.

So what exactly can the police do? The square is filled with Serbian families out for a stroll. They cannot arrest all of them. They cannot even arrest the paying bat-swingers who have potentially disrespected a public official. Striking a picture on a drum is a pretty weak charge. Also, police need to be serious and intimidating. They would look ridiculous reacting so strongly to something like this. Whoever made the contraption is no-where to be found. So what did the police finally do? What did they finally arrest and take into custody? The barrel, of course.

About fifteen Serbian youth were behind this humorous protest against the then Serbian dictator. Srdja Popovic was one of those youths. In his TEDx talk "The Power of Laughtivism," Popovic uses this experience from his own life to talk about the power of using laughter to bring about social and political change. Popovic gives three reasons why protests that use humor can be uniquely effective. The first reason is that "Humor melts fear."[1] For Popovic, it is fear that oppressive governments use to keep power. Fear forces citizens to stay in line and to do all that they can to stay on the government's good side. Popovic switches his metaphor when he says that fear is the air that dictators breathe. Humor has the unique ability to eliminate fear, to suck out all of that air. Put another way, humor changes a dictator's oxygen to carbon monoxide. It also replaces the fear, the carbon monoxide that citizens find, and gives citizens fearless, life-giving oxygen. Popovic's second reason is that such humorous protests make a movement look cool and thereby attract attention and interest. People, especially young people, want to be part of things that are cool. The third reason is what Popovic describes as the huge dilemma that humorous protests create for serious, frightening, oppressive regimes. The dilemma is that if those re-gimes respond forcefully to humorous protests, then the contrast between a light, funny protest and a serious or brutal crackdown puts the dictatorship in its harshest light. But if oppressive governments do not respond, they risk looking ridiculous and losing credibility. Lack of government response may encourage others to resist.

Most of Popovic's TED talk highlights examples of humorous protests with people from places like Montenegro, Iran, and Egypt using laughter to bring about positive political change. Besides those examples, we can turn to another contemporary way people use laughter to encourage posi-tive change: political cartoons. The example given here is by Liza Donnelly. Donnelly's cartoon shows an easy-to-recognize scene of two girls playing together with dolls (figure 5).

---

1. Tedx Talks, "Power of Laughtivism," 3:16–3:20.

*"I can't decide what I want to be when I
grow up: a good girl or a slut."*

Figure 5. Donnelly, Liza. "*I Can't Decide What I Want to Be When I
Grow Up: A Good Girl or a Slut.*" **Used by permission of the artist.**

Perhaps the dolls got one of the girls thinking about when she would
be an adult. Part of what makes it funny is that we don't expect such a young
girl to understand the terrible dilemma so many women feel.

Can You Understand Laughter Activism without This Guy? No, You Kant

What does Donnelly's cartoon about a young girl deciding to be a good girl
or a slut have to do with Popovic's ideas about laughter activism? What do
they share in common, and how might they try to make the world a better
place? To get at that, we will use the insights of Immanuel Kant.

Kant was an important German thinker in the late 1700s. He remains
important today because once you start to study him, you soon realize that
even philosophers now just Kant get enough of him. Of course a lot of

first-year students Kant stand the guy! And lots of talentless writers just Kant help themselves from making puns on the way that his last name is similar to the word "can't." But those aren't the only reasons he's important. As you'll see, we Kant really understand laughter activism without him.

What makes us laugh, according to Kant, is when something very out of the ordinary disrupts our expectations. This something out of the ordinary cannot just be anything. If that were the case, we'd laugh whenever we were surprised. Not everything that is surprising makes us laugh, but for Kant laughter always has an element of surprise. The word Kant uses for that surprising element is "absurd." What Kant says then is that "in everything that is to excite a lively convulsive laugh there must be something absurd."[2]

But for Kant, laughter isn't just the joy of being surprised by something absurd. Kant describes what is happening when we laugh. And what is happening is we are being tricked. We are expecting one thing and getting something else. Kant says in order to make us laugh, the joke or the "jest must contain something that is capable of deceiving for a moment."[3] This is the part where we are tricked. What happens next is we suddenly realize we've been tricked. Kant's phrase for this is that the "illusion is dissipated."[4] After we realize we were tricked, Kant says "the mind turns back to try it once again."[5] We think about the set-up and the trick, and we play back the surprise over and over again. We switch rapidly between what we believed and what the truth turned out to be. Again, Kant's way to say that is "thus through a rapidly alternating tension and relaxation [our thinking] is jerked back and put into a state of oscillation."[6] Oscillation means it goes back and forth. What is going back and forth here is our mind switching rapidly between set-up and surprise.

To see what Kant has in mind, we return to Liza Donnelly's cartoon. Donnelly is counting on viewers focusing first on what they see. You look at the girls playing, and you see one is speaking to the other. You notice that they are sitting on the floor together in a bedroom. You guess that they are elementary school age, if not younger. From what you see, you make some predictions about what the one girl with her mouth open is saying to the other. If you walked by the bedroom door, saw the girls playing, and

2. Kant, "Critique of Judgment," 47.

3. Kant, "Critique of Judgment," 48.

4. Kant, "Critique of Judgment," 48.

5. Kant, "Critique of Judgment," 48.

6. Kant, "Critique of Judgment," 48.

noticed one was speaking, you would probably predict that she might be saying something related to the dolls. She might be asking for the red boots or saying that they should pretend that the dolls are going on a trip to the beach. Donnelly then counts on you reading the caption. It is in quotation marks, so you know it is supposed to be what one girl is telling her friend. What you don't expect is for the girl to casually throw out that she is trying to decide which of society's two terrible paths she will choose. Donnelly and Kant are counting on you incorrectly predicting what the girl says to her playmate. They also count on you understanding the awful choice the girl is considering. They count on you feeling surprised at this unexpected twist. Kant predicts you will go back and forth between what you expected the girl might say and what she actually says. Donnelly plans on you also going back and forth between the terrible choice women too often face and a very young girl already seeing it. The surprises cause laughter. That laughter stretches out as you mentally go back and forth between what you expected and what you got.

Gautier "Spends Time" with a Grand Odalisque

In 1855, the French author and art critic Théophile Gautier went to the "Exposition Universelle." This world's fair was very, very popular. Over five million people attended. The event featured the best in agriculture, industry, and the fine arts from twenty-seven countries. The exhibition's fine arts area included paintings by some of the most important artists of the time. One of those works, the *Grand Odalisque*, was painted by Jean-Auguste-Dominique Ingres (figure 6). Yes, this is the same Ingres that I talked about in chapter four about Picasso and Braque. Oh, and yes, I am again using his fine but unfunny painting as a set up.

Gautier was a very well-respected critic of the time. Today he is somewhat famous for his role as part of the creative team behind the ballet *Giselle*. So, yah, he's not that famous today. The "Exposition Universelle" ran from May to November of 1855, and in July of that year Gautier wrote his review of the art exhibition. His review was published in the influential French newspaper *Le Moniteur Universel*. In his review, Gautier had a lot to say about the *Grand Odalisque*. Before I get into Gautier's review, I want to make sure you know that an "odalisque" is a chambermaid, a female attendant, a concubine, or a sex slave owned by the sultan, pasha, or whatever else you want to call the guy who owns everything in the palace. Ingres shows this woman in a private space surrounded by objects associated with a harem.

Figure 6. Ingres, Jean Auguste Dominique. 1814. *Grand Odalisque.*
Paris, Musée du Louvre. Photo Credit: Scala/Art Resource, NY.

Gautier's review of Ingres's painting is absolutely glowing. He goes so far as to say that the paintbrush never made anything more perfect than this painting. He describes the woman in the painting as a "divine beauty" who is displaying her "chaste nudity to the eyes of men unworthy of contemplating her."[7] We could surmise that Gautier, a man, would also be unworthy, but he must have thought he got some sort of pass, because then he takes time to contemplate each part of her divine beauty and chaste nudity. The woman is "half raised on her elbow buried in pillows."[8] The way her head turns toward the viewer is a "movement full of grace."[9] As she moves, she "reveals shoulders of a golden whiteness."[10] We also see "a back in whose supple flesh runs a delicious serpentine line."[11] Gautier's idea is that her spine's elegant curve looks like a very, very tasty snake. As for the feet, Gautier notes that her "soles have only tread the carpets of Smyrna

7. Ockman, *Ingres's Eroticized Bodies*, 90.

8. Ockman, *Ingres's Eroticized Bodies*, 90.

9. Ockman, *Ingres's Eroticized Bodies*, 90.

10. Ockman, *Ingres's Eroticized Bodies*, 90.

11. Ockman, *Ingres's Eroticized Bodies*, 90.

or the steps of oriental alabaster in the pools of the harem."[12] This divine beauty doesn't have time for jogging or sweeping or chasing after children. In fact, Gautier is really into those feet. He describes how they "curve softly, fresh and white as camellia buds."[13] He adds that they seem to have been copies of ivory statues made by ancient Greek masters. Those are some feet!

Since Gautier has already told us that she is resting on her left arm, now he moves on to describe her right arm. He says it has been "languor-ously abandoned."[14] Languorously abandoned? I had to look up what lan-guorous means ("pleasantly tired" or "inert"). Her pleasantly tired arm is not only abandoned, but it "floats the length of the contour of the hips."[15] The right hand loosely holds a feather fan. But then Gautier returns to talk about the arm, saying it is separated enough from the body "to allow virgin breasts of exquisite form to be seen."[16] Of course that is not all he says about the breasts. He adds that they are "breasts of Greek Venus, sculpted by Cleomenes for the temple of Cyprus."[17] Like the feet, those beautiful breasts seem copied from ancient Greek masters. But this woman and her breasts are not in ancient Greece. Instead, she has been "transported to the harem of a pasha."[18] It is unclear exactly how she was transported. I'm guessing she was probably transported there by UPS or the naked-golden-white-ideal-feet-and-breasts-sex-slave delivery service that was popular back then. Maybe they used Lusty Lyft? Or Uber Hottie?

Okay, I tried, I mean I really tried to be serious through this descrip-tion. Part of what makes Gautier's review so ridiculous to me is how over-the-top and flowery it seems. The review seems like the purple prose that someone like Ignatius from *A Confederacy of Dunces* would like. It also sounds like he's trying to use ancient Greek art to explain why this painting turns him on so much. But what is really making this ridiculous to me is how voyeuristic it sounds. "Voyeuristic" is a term you can use at a party when you actually want to say "pervy." This French poet is looking at this nude sex slave like he is the pasha and she is an object he gets to use and enjoy. She is not a person with a reality to acknowledge and respect. She

12. Ockman, *Ingres's Eroticized Bodies*, 90.

13. Ockman, *Ingres's Eroticized Bodies*, 90.

14. Ockman, *Ingres's Eroticized Bodies*, 90.

15. Ockman, *Ingres's Eroticized Bodies*, 90.

16. Ockman, *Ingres's Eroticized Bodies*, 90.

17. Ockman, *Ingres's Eroticized Bodies*, 90.

18. Ockman, *Ingres's Eroticized Bodies*, 90.

is beautiful body parts he gets to visually consume like a buffet. And the problem isn't just that he gets to consume her. The problem is that Gautier's language makes it sound like she is delighted and sexually satisfied. When he says "languorously abandoned," he's talking about her right arm. The arm floats along the contour of the hips. This tells us that not just her arm, but her whole body is pleasantly tired or inert. Why is it pleasantly tired? Gautier invites us to conclude that her body is pleasantly tired because it has sexually abandoned itself and allowed itself to float in the pleasure of the pasha's (or the sultan's or the viewer's) sexual gratification.

There is one more thing to consider about this painting and Gautier's response. Gautier is a French man at a world's fair. Sure, part of the idea of the fair is to let people from all over the world show what they have to offer in areas like agriculture, industry, and the fine arts. But the French people paying for this and most of the French people going to this are showing off what they offer to the rest of the world. In the thinking of the time, France was an advanced and industrial country. Other places were not as advanced. France had the opportunity, maybe even the burden, to help less-advanced people and societies develop to become like France. France and other European countries had colonies to do just that. European countries used their colonies to develop the resources of those places, and this development helped the colonies and the Europeans. French and other European colonies were in places that had harems, places like Morocco, Algeria, and the Middle East. When we keep all of this in mind—how France saw itself as advanced and saw colonialism as a responsibility and an opportunity—then we can see Gautier taking advantage of this opportunity. Not only does he get to imagine that he's the sultan or pasha, but he also does this while patting himself on the back for being from a society more advanced than that of any sultan or pasha. Gautier and other male viewers contemplate the *Grand Odalisque* and visually enjoy the sexually available and sexually satisfied slave. They also enjoy the privilege of being from a powerful, advanced society. These men use this painting at this world's fair to enjoy at their pleasure the sex slave, her exotic location, and their French male superiority over the sultan. Everything about this painting flatters the cultural and racial superiority and the sexist male fantasies of men like Gautier.[19]

19. Said, *Orientalism*.

Women Taking Swings and Melting Fear

All of the reasons I dislike what Gautier gets out of the *Grand Odalisque*—
how it flatters cultural and racial superiority while feeding sexist male fantasies—are why I love these next two works.

The Guerrilla Girls' poster, *Do Women Have to Be Naked to Get into
the Met. Museum?*, uses Ingres's *Grand Odalisque* (figure 7).

Figure 7. Guerrilla Girls. 1989. "*Do Women Have to Be Naked to Get
into the Met. Museum?*" **Used by permission of the artists.**

She is here because she is an easily recognizable female nude. Even
though she's in the Louvre, she is the sort of nude you'd find in the Metropolitan Museum of Art. The Guerrilla Girls also use her because she brings
with her all of the ideas we find in Gautier's review. She embodies how
men use her as an object of their sexual fantasies and cultural superiority. Even though she is cut away from her original background, and even
though now the sheet under her is a bright pink, we still have her tasty
snake spine, those amazing feet, and the breast—all of which were transported from ancient Greece to some harem. We have the "languorously
abandoned" arm along with the rest of the body. Of course making her
black-and-white means she's a little less visually delicious. Cut away from
that sumptuous background, she is a little less tasty and more difficult to
fantasize about. And that gorilla head really throws things off. Finally, there
is one more thing that seriously disrupts this fantasy—reading. Not only
do we not get the harem as our fantasy background, but we have this bright
yellow background and words. And those words aren't Gautier reading *50
Shades of Grey*. No, we have black, bold, block lettering, with a question
that reveals the sexism in the world around us. Below that question is more

reading, reading that answers the question with evidence and data about that sexism.

There is one more thing about this poster. In order to speak to people right now, the Guerrilla Girls use the visual language of advertising. They make this poster in many sizes, including billboard-sized. It is an excellent billboard because it uses bold colors, a simple and easy-to-take-in image, and straightforward, bold text. The image quickly grabs the audience's attention. Like all good advertising, its message can be taken in quickly, and the Guerrilla Girls want audiences to carry this message with them when they go to museums or galleries or when they see art anywhere. Where so much advertising encourages and feeds sexist fantasies, this work undercuts or subverts such fantasies.

Undercutting fantasies is also central to what Lalla Essaydi's 2008 photograph *Les Femmes de Maroc: Grande Odalisque* does. In January 2013, I was team-teaching a university class, and for part of the class we spent a week in Washington DC. I had never heard of Essaydi's work, but I went with another faculty member and some students to an exhibition at the National Museum of African Art. When I saw her large photographs from her *Les Femmes Du Maroc* series, I laughed.[20] Yes, they are beautiful photographs that represent great skill, insight, and hours of painstaking work, but I also find them very, very funny.

It is easy to see how Essaydi's version of the *Grand Odalisque* plays with the original. The figure's basic pose is the same as Ingres's figure, and there are pillows, sheets, and a curtain. Essaydi has removed the fan and the other objects surrounding the figure. She has changed her elaborate headdress for one that matches the surrounding fabrics. She has clothed the figure. The fabrics are a similar white color and material. Essaydi has also introduced four features that contrast sharply with the original—the Moroccan model, the setting, the calligraphic writing on almost every surface, and those dirty feet. For models, Essaydi uses friends and family members. The model here is a lovely, real person instead of an idealized "divine beauty." She is not a fantasy that is easily played with and exploited in one's mind. She is a person we can acknowledge and respect. She is also in a simple setting. She is not a beautiful object among many other beautiful objects. Instead, she is a person posing for a photograph.

Like the Guerrilla Girls' poster, Essaydi uses reading to interrupt fantasizing. Essaydi spends hours covering materials and models in ornate

20. See Essaydi and Mernissi, *Les Femmes Du Maroc*.

henna script. For Essaydi, this writing not only interrupts the male fantasies of an audience like Gautier but also gives the woman a voice. This writing is her thoughts and ideas. As the work includes the photographer's and the model's thoughts and ideas, it speaks back to whatever someone like Gautier might think, say, or write. The writing takes the voice and the power back from a male audience and gives it to the female artist and the model. A final element that takes power back are those dirty feet. These are not Greek marble statue feet or the feet of a woman who has only walked the carpets of Smyrna or rested in a chair poolside at the palace. These are the feet of someone who moves, who acts, who does things. These are the feet of someone with stuff to do. Carefully posed in this photograph, this woman is not languorously abandoned in a viewer's sexual fantasy. She imitates but rejects his fantasy, makes fun of it, shows its absurdity, and asserts that she is an active person and not a mere consumable object.

There is one more thing to say about Essaydi's parody of the *Grand Odalisque*. Essaydi is a Moroccan photographer with classical art training. She started as a painter. She has seen paintings like Ingres's over the many years she has been studying art. While she respects the skill that is evident in works like these, she sees the distance between these male fantasies and the north African reality. Essaydi grew up in a household where her father had four wives and she had many, many siblings. Her photographs, as discussed above, respond to the sexist fantasies that paintings like Ingres's encourage. Essaydi's work also responds to the racism. These women and their cultures are not inferior. They are not less advanced. It is not the responsibility or opportunity of powerful white men to develop or exploit them. Essaydi's photographs show the humanity of these Moroccan women. They invite viewers to acknowledge and respect that humanity.

Essaydi and the Guerrilla Girls take something that audiences know and throw in a surprise. Kant would say that they introduce something absurd. Audiences expect Ingres and Gautier. They expect a lush harem scene, a sumptuous nude, and a delightful stage for sexist and racist fantasies. In the poster and photograph, audiences are deceived, but only for a very small moment. The absurdity is the elements that undercut and subvert those fantasies. The original illusion is dissipated or dispelled in how the works reveal the ugly sexism and racism that were part of the original work. As Kant describes, the mind of the audience goes back and forth between the abuse and ugliness in the original and the witty cleverness of these two parodies. In fact, if you mentally switch back and forth between Ingres and the Guerrilla Girls/Essaydi fast enough, you can almost feel your mind and your body go "Ha-ha-ha-ha!"

What we get when we look at the Guerrilla Girls' and Essaydi's works are artists with a bat taking swings at an oil drum. On the drum is a color photocopy of Ingres's *Grand Odalisque*. With each clink and thud, with each public display of their art, they are melting fear. That fear is sexism's and racism's horrible power. That power forces women into two awful choices— good girl or slut. That power strips women of their full humanity. Donnelly, the Guerrilla Girls, and Essaydi humorously reveal that power. They use laughter to show its absurdity. That laughter, just as Popovic says, melts fear. These artists name the fears and make them look ridiculously foolish. They make the fight against racism and sexism look cool. They make it interesting and appealing. Laughter that names fear and encourages people to stand against those fears makes the world a better place.

CHAPTER 12

Nobody Here Is Leaving This Room a Better Person

"I DO THINK I have to quit comedy though."[1] That is what Hannah Gadsby announces in her Netflix special *Hannah Gadsby: Nanette*. Or at least she was thinking about it. One thing that holds her back from quitting is that she has a college degree in art history. If she quits comedy, she has no idea how she'd make a living with that degree. She cannot picture working in a gallery partly because galleries are highbrow. She says, "High art—that's what elevates and civilizes people."[2] Her idea is that things like galleries, ballet, and the theater edify you and make you a better person. She says this to set up this contrast: "Comedy—lowbrow. I'm sorry to inform you (but) nobody here is leaving this room a better person."[3] The timing and the cleverness of the contrast make it very funny. The joke fits well with Gadsby's other self-deprecating jokes. Gadsby might be right, but the rest of this chapter will argue that the opposite is true—many people would be leaving that room or wherever they watch *Hannah Gadsby: Nanette* a better person. To see how *Hannah Gadsby: Nanette* can make audiences better, we will first listen to an argument between two dead people and then look at a fictitious Little Rascal.

---

1. Parry and Olb, *Hannah Gadbsy*, 16:52–16:54.
2. Parry and Olb, *Hannah Gadbsy*, 32:11–32:13.
3. Parry and Olb, *Hannah Gadbsy*, 32:22–32:29.

Sarah's Invitation to Frank

You probably would not have thought anything of Sarah Smith from Goblers Green had you known her while she was alive. She was a run-of-the-mill woman. But that has changed since she died. Now she is majestic and glorious, the centerpiece in an extravagant procession that includes children and animals. In this place, Sarah is considered one of the great ones, and her brilliance comes from how her goodness reflects divine love.

Sarah is a heavenly being in C. S. Lewis's *The Great Divorce*. She has come to a place somewhere between heaven and what Lewis calls Grey Town to meet up with her husband. The "divorce" in Lewis's title is not about ending marriages. It is about separating spirits between those who choose heaven and those who choose something else. Sarah is here to invite Frank to follow her to heaven. Where Sarah is filled with light that radiates from her, Frank is quite different. He has come up from Grey Town, but he is an immaterial little ghost called the Dwarf. Frank has a tall, thin, and shaky black puppet that he carries with him, a puppet that he works like a ventriloquist dummy. That puppet is known as the Tragedian, and it is an appropriate name because it expresses Frank's dramatic self-regard and self-pity.

The first thing Sarah does when she meets Frank is apologize for her shortcomings while she was alive. Frank does not meet her affectionate gaze. Instead, he uses the Tragedian to offer an empty and arrogant "We'll say no more about it. We all make mistakes."[4] Frank then redirects the conversation down the track he'd like it to take. He says that during the time that they've been separated, his greatest concern was that her heart was absolutely breaking without him. It turns out that it wasn't. Sarah has been in heaven, and there she has experienced a fullness of divine love. She cannot explain that to Frank right now, so, when he says that she must have been a long time heartbroken, she tells him that all of that is over now. Sarah knows Frank's self-pitying tendency, but instead of addressing that tendency directly, she wants to point him toward the full joy he can now begin to experience.

Sadly, Frank does not allow Sarah's redirection. Frank returns to what he wants to address by asking her, in a bleating voice, "You missed me?"[5] Sarah again tries to redirect Frank to the joy that awaits him, but when she does not answer his question, Frank and his ventriloquist dummy jump on

4. Lewis, *Great Divorce*, 122.
5. Lewis, *Great Divorce*, 123.

that fact. Frank uses the Tragedian to theatrically pose the question again: "You missed me?"[6] When she again evades the question, promising him happiness and the chance to leave such sorrow behind, Frank and the Tragedian launch into a speech about how wonderful they would be if they dropped the question. They pat themselves on the back for what they might do, but then they remind themselves of all the things they did for Sarah while alive that went overlooked and unappreciated. As they continue bemoaning the many miseries they have suffered, Sarah chimes in that she wants to take them to a place where there are no miseries. For a moment, Frank seems drawn to the idea, but then the Tragedian says, "Look here" and "We've got to face this."[7] The narrator adds that the Tragedian "was using his 'manly' bullying tone this time: the one for bringing women to their senses."[8] Sarah is not cowed by this chauvinistic treatment. She tells Frank that the reason he wants her to say she missed him is because that would show him that she loved him. She promises Frank there is a better way to love. Frank melodramatically questions if she has any idea what love really is, and she replies that she does now. Since Sarah has lived in heaven, she has experienced love. That love is of a much stronger intensity and magnitude. She says mortal love has more to do with needing. Perplexed, Frank asks her if she needs him anymore. When Sarah tells him that no, she does not need him any longer, she promises a life and love that are far superior to what they had before.

Frank cannot grasp the invitation that Sarah is extending. He cannot imagine living without misery and self-pity. He cannot imagine love that is not needing and needy. Frank and the Tragedian respond to Sarah's invitation with another extended, melodramatic pity party. They say that they would have rather seen Sarah die at their feet than for things to have ended in this sorry state. Sarah allows this to pointlessly continue for a bit, but then stops it by saying, "Look at me. Look at me. What are you doing with that great, ugly doll? Let go of the chain. Send it away. It is you I want. Don't you see what nonsense it's talking?"[9] Sarah invites Frank to get rid of his dummy and the self-pity it embodies. She brings Frank back to reality by pointing out that being dramatic about death in this place doesn't do him any good. He did see her dying, but it wasn't at their feet. It was in a nursing

6. Lewis, *Great Divorce*, 123.

7. Lewis, *Great Divorce*, 125.

8. Lewis, *Great Divorce*, 125.

9. Lewis, *Great Divorce*, 126.

home. She goes on, "a very good nursing home it was too. Matron would never have dreamed of leaving bodies lying about the floor!"[10]

Sarah takes what Frank and the Tragedian said, turns it around, and shows the ridiculousness of it. She makes a joke, and her joke is meant to snap Frank back to reality. The key moment in this episode is when the narrator describes how Sarah does this. The narration reads, "Merriment danced in her eyes. She was sharing a joke with the Dwarf, right over the head of the Tragedian. Something not at all unlike a smile struggled to appear on the Dwarf's face. For he was looking at her now. Her laughter was past his first defenses."[11] Sarah, who is full of joy and love, invites Frank to put down his self-pity and other defenses and follow her into heaven. She makes this invitation with the merriment that dances in her eyes and with the joke that gets around Frank's defensive self-pity.

Sarah's invitation in the form of a joke, her laughter that gets past Frank's first defenses, is an excellent example of Hutcheson's idea of the power of joking, or ridicule, in a wise woman's hands. Her joke was an edged tool that momentarily cut through Frank's blinding self-pity. This is also a moment when Frank genuinely sees Sarah. He avoided her gaze before and spoke with her indirectly. The joy and comfort Sarah's laughter offered had the power to draw Frank into really seeing her.

Hominy Jenkins

Sarah's merriment, joke, and laughter draw Frank into finally looking at her and seeing her. A similar idea comes through in the novel discussed in chapter 6 and its discussion of Paul Beatty's novel *The Sellout*. The novel's narrator, Bonbon, has a neighbor, Hominy Jenkins, who used to be one of the Little Rascals. That narrator has a complicated relationship with Hominy. Again, I'll let you read the novel yourself because it would sound odd if I tried to explain it here.

Toward the end of the novel, Bonbon reflects on Hominy and his life. When we meet him, Hominy is long past his prime and shows signs of Alzheimer's. Bonbon and Hominy attend a screening of some of Hominy's Little Rascals movies. Bonbon is struck by Hominy's skill in taking his part, a part where he is the butt of ugly racist episodes and jokes. Bonbon reflects on what it must have been like for a young black actor to be successful in a

10. Lewis, *Great Divorce*, 127.
11. Lewis, *Great Divorce*, 126–27.

very racist environment. He says, "Sometimes I forget how funny Hominy is. Back in the day, to avoid the succession of booby traps laid by the white man, black people had to constantly be thinking on their feet."[12] Not only did the young Hominy need to be quick on his feet, but Bonbon goes on that, "You had to be ready with an impromptu quip or a down-home bromide that would disarm and humble a white provocateur."[13] It is during this reflection that Bonbon says something important for this chapter and this book: "Maybe if your sense of humor reminded him there was a semblance of humanity underneath that burrhead, you might avoid a beating, get some of that back pay you were owed."[14] What the young Hominy learned, and what bullied and oppressed people everywhere see, is that if the bully or oppressor can see the humanity of others, and especially their victims, then the situation might change. Humor can get around the blinding defenses that biased or bigoted views create. Humor becomes an invitation to live better, to see others better, and to be better connected with them. Humor as an invitation to connection is precisely what makes *Hannah Gadsby: Nanette* so powerful.

Nanette

The first few minutes of *Hannah Gadsby: Nanette* are light and easy to watch. Gadsby talks about naming her show and about how she often feels uncomfortable in small towns. Hannah is rather tall, with short, dark hair, glasses, and a sharp blue suit. In a small town, people initially mistake her for a man, but when they realize they were mistaken, that is when her discomfort sets in. With these initial jokes, Gadsby places front-and-center the way that she seems "gender not normal."[15] She does this in a way that is not distressing. She relieves some of the tension that the audience might initially feel. But don't worry, we'll get plenty of that tension later.

The easy, comfortable way that Gadsby starts her show is like a Trojan horse. When the ancient Greeks could not break into Troy, they tricked the Trojans by saying they were leaving. They offered a large wooden horse as a sort of "sorry-for-attacking-killing-and-trying-to-destroy-you-for-ten-years-our-bad" gift. The Trojans accepted the gift and brought it into the city.

12. Beatty, *Sellout*, 243.
13. Beatty, *Sellout*, 243.
14. Beatty, *Sellout*, 243.
15. Parry and Olb, *Hannah Gadbsy*, 19:15.

Inside the horse were Greek soldiers who got out of the horse at night and opened the city gates so that the rest of the Greek army could defeat the Trojans and sack their city. The way Gadsby starts her show, the way the jokes put an audience at ease, causes that audience to lower their guard and accept the gift Gadsby offers. What hops out of this gift, what comes out in the course of the show, are sharp criticisms of the sexism and homophobia that still have so much power in the world. Gadsby's most powerful soldiers that work to defeat sexism and homophobia are laughter, contrasts, and stories.

Hannah Gadsby: Nanette is very, very funny. She has many years of experience at what she does, and has honed her craft to a very high level. Much of what makes it funny are her confidence on stage, her tone, her timing, her facial expressions, and the overall ways she presents the material. Those elements cannot be captured here. In fact, my singular hope is that my arguments will be persuasive enough that you will watch the show, laugh at how brilliantly funny it is, and enjoy it more because of the insights I offer.

What you find in *Hannah Gadsby: Nanette* are a number of powerful contrasts. Toward the beginning of the show, Gadsby mentions a story she told early in her comedy career about a man who mistook her for someone flirting with his girlfriend. It is a funny story about mistaken identity. When Gadsby returns to this story much later in the show, she uses it to illustrate the darkest sides of homophobia and sexism. This contrast flips what had seemed like a light, funny story. Another powerful contrast in the show also involves sexism, homophobia, and violence. Gadsby makes a joke toward the beginning about the ugly, sexist comments made to women who are too sensitive. The comments are that such women need to not be so sensitive and that they need to relax. Ugly sexual violence is touted as something that might help them relax and be less sensitive. Later in the show, Gadsby talks about what a difficult time it might be for straight, white men. Such men suddenly find their power being questioned. She mentions how angry and upset such men are becoming. She comments that perhaps they are just being too sensitive. Perhaps they just need to relax. At that she brings back the ugly advice about sexual violence as a cure or aid. This contrast further demonstrates the idea's horrific absurdity.

There is another contrast that makes this show powerful. Gadsby talks about her background in art history. She talks about Vincent Van Gogh, his struggles, and his important relationship with his brother. This important, healthy, and mutually reinforcing relationship contrasts sharply with the abusive relationship Picasso had with Marie-Thérèse Walter. Picasso embodies all of the ugly sexism that Gadsby criticizes. Gadsby using comedy to attack abusive male power contrasts with something else she describes—how comedians took pot shots at Monica Lewinsky instead of using their power against Bill Clinton.

The final contrast brings us to the importance of stories for Gadsby. Again at the beginning of the show, Gadsby mentions her story of coming out to her mother. This is a story she has told since the early part of her career, and it is very funny. When she returns to the story later in the show, we get a very different spin and outcome. The first version delightfully makes fun of her mother's homophobic response. The second version is a moving account of how her mother has changed over time. It is a powerful expression of growth and love. Gadsby uses this and other stories to highlight how comedy can overemphasize tension and how it can leave out some of the most important parts. This leads Gadsby to conclude that "stories hold our cure" for the sexism, homophobia, anger, and disconnection that make the world so awful.[16] She does not view laughter itself as the cure; laughter is "the honey that sweetens the bitter medicine."[17] Often stories can be hard to hear. This is especially true if you have been part of the problem, part of the system that caused so much pain or at least benefited from it. Gadsby concludes her show with a reference to Van Gogh's sunflowers: "Do you know why we have the sunflowers? It's not because Vincent van Gogh suffered. It's because Vincent van Gogh had a brother who loved him. Through all the pain, he had a tether, a connection to the world. And that is the focus of the story we need. Connection."[18]

In contrast with what she said, I believe Gadsby wants everyone who watches her show to leave a better person. She seems to imagine at least two audiences. One audience is those who have been bullied, and especially other abused "not normals" like her. Part of the value of sharing her story in such a funny and public manner is its tremendous benefits for people passing through experiences like hers. At the beginning of the show, she mentions how difficult it was to make sense of her experiences in a world that at best had no place for someone like her. After sharing her experiences, this is what she says about the value of her story for people like her: "What I would have done to have heard a story like mine, not for blame, not

16. Parry and Olb, *Hannah Gadsby*, 1:06:55.
17. Parry and Olb, *Hannah Gadsby*, 1:06:56–1:06:59.
18. Parry and Olb, *Hannah Gadsby*, 1:07:41–1:08:06.

for reputation, not for money, not for power, but to feel less alone, to feel connected."[19] Gadsby's story, enlivened and sweetened by laughter, powerfully lifts and encourages those audiences.

A second audience is straight, white men. Gadsby lulls them into a false comfort at the beginning of the show and increases their tension as it goes along. She attacks permissive attitudes toward sexual violence. She shows the ugly sides of sexism and homophobia. She attacks how powerful abusive men and the society that supports them value a famous man's reputation over the suffering of others. Gadsby recognizes that she has been attacking many of the sexist assumptions that support male power. She comes right out and says, "To the men in the room . . . who feel I may have been persecuting you this evening . . . well spotted. That's pretty much what I've done there."[20] But Gadsby clarifies that one of the reasons she has done this was to give men a small taste of what she has experienced during her life. Straight, white men may have been singled out, clumped together with other straight, white men who are actually quite different from them, and then accused of some of society's worst evils, but that pain has neither the intensity nor duration of what "not normals" constantly experience.

Hannah Gadsby: Nanette uses laughter and stories to send a powerful invitation. That invitation is to see Gadsby and people like her better. It is an invitation to recognize their humanity. Gadsby's jokes are like what Bonbon said about black comedians—they remind audiences that there is a humanity underneath any external differences. Gadsby's laughter, or the laughter she inspires in audiences, can get past first defenses. Those defenses include the many ways sexism and homophobia are justified or excused. Gadsby brings up those defensive tactics, like accusing the abused of being too sensitive and telling them that they need to lighten up. *Hannah Gadbsy: Nanette* shows how absurdly ridiculous it is to tell the abused to not get upset about their abuse. Gadsby is like Sarah Smith. Gadsby, who is full of strength and resilience, invites audiences to set aside ugly, sexist, homophobic, and abusive ways of looking and living and to instead follow her to a place of compassionate connection.

Hannah Gadsby: Nanette is a form of laughter activism. Gadsby's stories and the laughter she uses to sweeten their bitter medicine reduce fear. They cast frightening and abusive prejudices in such a light that we see them clearly. Seeing them clearly makes them less overwhelming. Gadsby

19. Parry and Olb, *Hannah Gadbsy*, 1:03:35–1:03:45.
20. Parry and Olb, *Hannah Gadbsy*, 1:05:30–1:05:44.

has tremendous power. In that respect, she gives another example of the power Tiffany Haddish describes in her memoir. Gadsby does not use her humor and power to shield innocent audiences, as Guido does for Giosuè. Gadsby uses that humor and power to attack the oppressive systems, but she also does something else. Like what Mateo does for his daughter Adi, Gadsby uses humor to educate and encourage people facing traumatic experiences. The undocumented Mateo's jokes educate and encourage his equally vulnerable daughter. Gadsby's humor speaks with compassion to lift and encourage young "not normals" like she once was. Gadsby's show is not populated with distant or defensive jokes that lift audiences out of their daily experiences and allow them to look down as if they were not involved. They are not the defense-mechanism jokes Freud describes. Gadsby's show honors and encourages the vulnerability that Brown describes and recommends. *Hannah Gadsby: Nanette* is powerful because Gadsby's vulnerability invites audiences to take those risks. To the degree that audiences take those risks, they enjoy much more than merely delightful laughter. They see others better and enjoy the connections that make life rich and satisfying.

Not Very Even-Handed Conclusion

What I Should Say

THE CONCLUSION TO THIS book about whether laughter can make the world a better place should be even-handed. It should bring together how no, laughter cannot make the world a better place, with maybe sometimes it can, and yes, it absolutely can. In fact, an even-handed conclusion could compare laughter to a hand. Like hands, laughter can pull someone up or push someone down. Laughter can strike, slap, staunch, or soothe. This conclusion should point out that laughter is one of a bully's most powerful weapons, it can widen the political divide, and it can release sexist attitudes and then behaviors. Laughter can reveal new possibilities, bring into question old ideas and values, and help you see your limitations. But revealing new possibilities does not mean you will see good possibilities. Questioning old ideas and values does not mean you will necessarily replace them with better ones. Laughter is just as prone to flatter your complacency as it is to encourage you to live better.

I should write an even-handed conclusion that assembles some of the most important points from the pages you've read, but the truth is that I don't see it that way. I'm a hopeful and optimistic soul. What gets me excited enough about laughter to study and write about it and to discuss it with my students is how laughter makes the world a better place. To make my uneven-handed concluding argument about how laughter makes the world a better place, I will say a bit more about *Hannah Gadsby: Nanette* and Paul Beatty's *The Sellout*. But before that, I will return to the discussion of Lewis's *The Great Divorce*.

Free Invitations

The previous discussion of *The Great Divorce* ended with Sarah Smith's invitation to her husband Frank to join her in heaven. Sarah's delightful and loving invitation got past Frank's first defenses. There is a bit more to the story. The narrator witnesses Frank's struggle "against joy."[1] The narrator concludes that "Somewhere, incalculable ages ago, there must have been gleams of humor and reason" in Frank.[2] Frank even momentarily sees the absurdity of what he's doing—"For one moment he did not at all misunderstand her laughter."[3] Then the narrator says something very sad: "But the light that reached him, reached him against his will. This was not the meeting he had pictured; he would not accept it."[4] Frank grabs the ropes of his grotesque Tragedian dummy and lashes out, "You dare to laugh at it!"[5]

In spite of Sarah's skill, compassion, and loving laughter, Frank does not accept her invitation. Audiences who watch *Hannah Gadsby: Nanette* or Hominy Jenkins in *The Sellout* do not have to accept their invitations. They do not have to be moved by Gadsby's jokes or comparisons or experiences. They do not have to be persuaded by Hominy's skills or antics. Audiences don't have to recognize their shared humanity with others. They do not have to connect. If the light that reaches such audiences is against their will, they can deploy new defenses and new means of self-justification to restore their abusive views, attitudes, and ways of living. So, if audiences can resist the connection and the positive transformations they are invited to make, why doesn't that put all of this in the "Maybe" section? If we cannot be sure that laughter's invitations to see and to live better will be accepted, then how exactly does laughter make the world a better place?

I believe part of the tremendous power of laughter's invitations is that they can be rejected. These are free invitations. They are not free for those who make them. Sarah Smith pays in the form of tremendous effort to extend her invitations. Hominy pays dearly as well, taking abuse but responding in his own humorous and gracious way. Hannah Gadsby has paid by developing her craft and then crafting her experiences into powerful, moving invitations. What is free is how an audience can accept the invitations or

1. Lewis, *Great Divorce*, 129.
2. Lewis, *Great Divorce*, 129.
3. Lewis, *Great Divorce*, 129.
4. Lewis, *Great Divorce*, 129.
5. Lewis, *Great Divorce*, 129.

not. This freedom acknowledges the humanity of the audience. In contrast, an invitation they would be forced to accept would not be an invitation. It would be a command. Human connection only happens when everyone involved is free to be connected or not, free to be open to the reality of another or free to ignore that reality. Laughter's free invitations offer two gifts. Laughter's invitations affirm the humanity of others. Laughter's invitations also provide breathtaking opportunities for the connections that make life richly satisfying. It is that double gift that makes the world better.

Bibliography

Allen, Andre. dir. *The Nightly Show with Larry Wilmore*. Season 1, episode 102, "Hillary Clinton's Emails; Kim Davis." Aired September 8, 2015, on Comedy Central.

Bakhtin, Mikhail. *Rabelais and His World*. Translated by Helene Iswolsky. Bloomington: Indiana University Press, 2009.

Beatty, Paul. *The Sellout*. New York: Farrar, Straus and Giroux, 2015.

Benigni, Roberto, dir. *Life Is Beautiful*. 1997. Rome: Melampo Cinematografica, Cecchi Gori Group Miramax.

Borges, Jorge Luis. *Other Inquisitions, 1937–1952*. Translated by Ruth L. C. Simms. Austin: University of Texas Press, 1964.

Brown, Brené. *Daring Greatly: How the Courage to Be Vulnerable Transforms the Way We Live, Love, Parent, and Lead*. New York: Avery, 2015.

Cloonan, William. "Braque's *Le Portugais* and a Portuguese Nun." *The French Review* 63.4 (1990) 607–16.

Cyrus, Miley. "My Way." Performed on *Saturday Night Live*. Season 41, episode 1. Aired October 3, 2015.

Danchev, Alex. *Georges Braque: A Life*. New York: Arcade, 2005.

Davis, Kim, et al. *Under God's Authority: The Kim Davis Story*. Orlando: New Revolution, 2018.

Einhorn, Randall. dir. *The Office*. Season 5, episode 19, "Golden Ticket." Aired March 12, 2009, in broadcast syndication, NBCUniversal.

Essaydi, Lalla, and Fatema Mernissi. *Les Femmes Du Maroc*. New York: powerHouse, 2009.

"Exercise Ball All the Way Over There." *The Onion*, December 5, 2007. https://www.theonion.com/excercise-ball-all-the-way-over-there-1819588811.

Fleischer, Ruben, dir. *Zombieland*. Culver City, CA: Columbia Pictures, 2009.

Ford, Thomas, et al. "Disparagement Humor and Prejudice: Contemporary Theory and Research." *Humor* 28 (May 1, 2015) 171–86.

———. "More Than 'Just a Joke': The Prejudice-Releasing Function of Sexist Humor." *Personality & Social Psychology Bulletin* 34 (March 1, 2008) 159–70. https://doi.org/10.1177/0146167207310022.

Ford, Thomas E., et al. "Sexist Humor as a Trigger of State Self-Objectification in Women." *Humor* 28.2 (May 1, 2015) 253–69.

Foucault, Michel. *The Order of Things: An Archaeology of the Human Sciences*. New York: Vintage, 1994.

Bibliography

Frascina, Francis. "Realism and Ideology: An Introduction to Semiotics and Cubism." In *Primitivism, Cubism, Abstraction: The Early Twentieth Century*, by Charles Harrison et al., 87–183. New Haven: Yale University Press, 1993.

Freud, Sigmund. "Humour." In *The Philosophy of Laughter and Humor*, edited by John Morreall, 111–16. Albany, NY: SUNY Press, 1986.

Friedenthal, Richard. *Letters of the Great Artists*. New York: Random House, 1963.

Funny Or Die. "Clerks and Recreation with Kim Davis." *YouTube*, September 4, 2015. Video, 1:09. https://www.youtube.com/watch?v=Wiu88238g0A.

———. "Kim Davis Met the Pope on PopeMeet.Com." *YouTube*, October 1, 2015. Video, 1:54. https://www.youtube.com/watch?v=v23YzJtp1_8.

Gallo, Sarah. "Humor in Father-Daughter Immigration Narratives of Resistance." *Anthropology & Education Quarterly* 47.3 (September 2016) 279–96. https://doi.org/10.1111/aeq.12156.

Haddish, Tiffany. *The Last Black Unicorn*. New York: Gallery, 2017.

Horvitz, Louis J., dir. *The 67th Primetime Emmy Awards*. Music. Academy of Television Arts and Sciences, Don Mischer Productions, 2015.

Hurley, Matthew M., et al. *Inside Jokes: Using Humor to Reverse-Engineer the Mind*. Cambridge, MA: MIT Press, 2013.

Hutcheson, Francis. "Reflections upon Laughter." In *The Philosophy of Laughter and Humor*, edited by John Morreall, 26–40. Albany, NY: SUNY Press, 1986.

K., Adrienne. "Harvard's 'Conquistabros and Navajos' Frat Party." *Native Appropriations*, October 21, 2010. https://nativeappropriations.com/2010/10/harvards-conquistabros-and-navajos-frat-party.html.

Kant, Immanuel. "Critique of Judgment." In *The Philosophy of Laughter and Humor*, edited by John Morreall, 45–50. Albany, NY: SUNY Press, 1986.

Kubrick, Stanley. dir. *Dr. Strangelove or: How I Learned to Stop Worrying and Love the Bomb*. Culver City, CA: Columbia Pictures, 1964.

Lauer, Peter, dir. *Malcolm in the Middle*. Season 7, episode 1, "Burning Man." Aired September 30, 2005, in broadcast syndication, on FOX.

Lewis, C. S. *The Great Divorce: A Dream*. New York: HarperOne, 2009.

Lieberman, Matthew D. *Social: Why Our Brains Are Wired to Connect*. New York: Crown, 2013.

McNeil, Taylor. "Everyone's a Comedian." *Tufts Now*, April 6, 2012. https://now.tufts.edu/articles/everyone-as-comedian.

Menken, Alan, and Stephen Schwartz. "Topsy-Turvy." Track 3 on *The Hunchback of Notre Dame: An Original Walt Disney Records Soundtrack*. Released May 28, 1996, Walt Disney Records.

Miller, Arthur. *Death of a Salesman*. Rev. ed. Edited by Gerald Weales. Harmondsworth, UK: Penguin, 1996.

Moya-Smith, Simon. "'Colonial Bros and Nava-Hos' Frat Party Investigated by California University." *NBC News*, November 22, 2013. http://www.nbcnews.com/news/us-news/colonial-bros-nava-hos-frat-party-investigated-california-university-flna2D11644720.

"New Starbucks Opens in Rest Room of Existing Starbucks." *The Onion*, June 27, 1998. https://www.theonion.com/new-starbucks-opens-in-rest-room-of-existing-starbucks-1819564800.

Bibliography

"Nobel Fever Grips Research Community as Prize Swells To $190 Million." *The Onion*, June 20, 2001. https://www.theonion.com/nobel-fever-grips-research-community-as-prize-swells-to-1819566095.

Ockman, Carol. *Ingres's Eroticized Bodies: Retracing the Serpentine Line*. New Haven: Yale University Press, 1995.

Parry, Madeleine, and John Olb, dirs. *Hannah Gadsby: Nanette*. Los Gatos, CA: Netflix, 2018.

Rensin, Emmett. "The Smug Style in American Liberalism." *Vox*, April 21, 2016. https://www.vox.com/2016/4/21/11451378/smug-american-liberalism.

Reynolds, Gene. dir. *M*A*S*H*. Season 1, episode 1, "Pilot." Aired September 17, 1972, in broadcast syndication, on 20th Century Fox.

Richardson, John, and Marilyn McCully. *A Life of Picasso*. New York: Knopf, 2007.

Said, Edward W. *Orientalism*. London: Penguin, 2007.

The School of Life. "Humour in Relationships." *YouTube*, 2016. Video, 4:51. https://www.youtube.com/watch?v=ehIiWha1oU8.

Siegfried, Susan L. *Ingres: Painting Reimagined*. New Haven: Yale University Press, 2009.

TEDx Talks. "The Power of Laughtivism: Srdja Popovic at TEDxBG." *YouTube*, 2013. Video, 13:12. https://www.youtube.com/watch?v=BgaDUcttL2s.

Toole, John Kennedy. *A Confederacy of Dunces*. New York: Grove, 1987.

Wemp, Brian. "Social Space, Technology, and Consumer Culture at the Grands Magasins Dufayel." *Historical Reflections/Réflexions Historiques* 37.1 (March 1, 2011) 1–17. https://doi.org/10.3167/hrrh.2011.370101.

Wilbur, Christopher J., and Lorne Campbell. "Humor in Romantic Contexts: Do Men Participate and Women Evaluate?" *Personality and Social Psychology Bulletin* 37.7 (July 1, 2011) 918–29. https://doi.org/10.1177/0146167211405343.

Wittebols, James H. *Watching M*A*S*H, Watching America: A Social History of the 1972–1983 Television Series*. Jefferson, NC: McFarland, 1998.

Wright, Steven. "Ants." Track 2 on *I Have a Pony*. Released in 1985, Warner Bros. Records.

Index

Index

Index